Cambridge Elements

Elements in Women in Music
edited by
Rhiannon Mathias
Bangor University

JULIE REISSEROVÁ (1888–1938)

Czech Composer and Feminist

Jean-Paul C. Montagnier
University of Lorraine

Shaftesbury Road, Cambridge CB2 8EA, United Kingdom

One Liberty Plaza, 20th Floor, New York, NY 10006, USA

477 Williamstown Road, Port Melbourne, VIC 3207, Australia

314–321, 3rd Floor, Plot 3, Splendor Forum, Jasola District Centre, New Delhi – 110025, India

103 Penang Road, #05–06/07, Visioncrest Commercial, Singapore 238467

Cambridge University Press is part of Cambridge University Press & Assessment, a department of the University of Cambridge.

We share the University's mission to contribute to society through the pursuit of education, learning and research at the highest international levels of excellence.

www.cambridge.org
Information on this title: www.cambridge.org/9781009517362

DOI: 10.1017/9781009411080

© Jean-Paul C. Montagnier 2025

This publication is in copyright. Subject to statutory exception and to the provisions of relevant collective licensing agreements, no reproduction of any part may take place without the written permission of Cambridge University Press & Assessment.

When citing this work, please include a reference to the DOI 10.1017/9781009411080

First published 2025

A catalogue record for this publication is available from the British Library

ISBN 978-1-009-51736-2 Hardback
ISBN 978-1-009-41106-6 Paperback
ISSN 2633-6871 (online)
ISSN 2633-6863 (print)

Cambridge University Press & Assessment has no responsibility for the persistence or accuracy of URLs for external or third-party internet websites referred to in this publication and does not guarantee that any content on such websites is, or will remain, accurate or appropriate.

Julie Reisserová (1888–1938)

Czech Composer and Feminist

Elements in Women in Music

DOI: 10.1017/9781009411080
First published online: January 2025

Jean-Paul C. Montagnier
University of Lorraine

Author for correspondence: Jean-Paul C. Montagnier,
jean-paul.montagnier@univ-lorraine.fr

Abstract: Regarded as the "first Czech woman composer of importance" by the *Grove Dictionary* in 1954, Julie Reisserová's name has since virtually disappeared from the musical and musicological landscape. Reisserová, one of Albert Roussel's most famous Czech students during the interwar period, was not only a successful composer in her time, but also an active feminist. Her music was generally well received and performed by prestigious musicians. The only comprehensive study of her life and work, published in 1948, was written by Jiřina Vacková. If Vacková was able to investigate the personal archives of the diplomat Jan Reisser – Reisserová's husband – before they were seized and/or destroyed by the communist regime, her book remains hagiographical. This Element draws up a new biographical sketch of the artist, reviews Reisserová's thoughts on the status of women composers between the wars, considers the reception of her six surviving scores, and examines her style.

Keywords: Julie Reisserová, woman composer, Czech music, feminism, women's studies

© Jean-Paul C. Montagnier 2025

ISBNs: 9781009517362 (HB), 9781009411066 (PB), 9781009411080 (OC)
ISSNs: 2633-6871 (online), 2633-6863 (print)

Contents

1 Introduction   1

2 Biographical Sketch   5

3 Reisserová and Feminism   22

4 Musical Works   35

5 Stylistic Considerations   52

6 Conclusion   63

Appendix A: Vienna Lecture (1937)   65

Appendix B: Catalog of Musical Works   69

Appendix C: List of Documented Public Performances of Reisserová's Music   72

Select Bibliography   80

1 Introduction

Celebrated and recognized in her time, the name of Julie Reisserová (Figure 1) gradually faded after World War II, and the political changes that followed in Eastern Europe. The main triggering factor probably occurred in South America.

On May 25, 1946, a Pan American World Airways plane landed at Santos Dumont airport, Rio de Janeiro. On board, the new Czech ambassador Jan Reisser and his legation were about to set foot in Brazil.[1] Yet, what Reisser – appointed to replace Vladimír Noseck, who because of his democratic opinions had become suspect and had been summoned to Prague a month earlier – and his second wife, the soprano Marie Bodláková-Reisserová, could not imagine was that they were going to spend the rest of their life there.[2] With the coup d'état of February 21–25, 1948, by which the Communist Party of Czechoslovakia took control of the government, and the mysterious death of the Foreign Minister Jan Masaryk, Reisser was placed under the strict supervision of a member of the party. His position becoming untenable, he announced on March 18, 1949, that he could no longer serve the new regime in his country, and then resigned and asked the Brazilian government to grant him and Marie Bodláková-Reisserová asylum.[3] As a result, he became persona non grata, and the music of his *first* spouse, Julie Reisserová (who passed away eleven years earlier), was banned from public performance in the Czechoslovak Socialist Republic. The personal papers and archives of the Reissers, which remained in their Prague home,[4] were very likely seized – as were the belongings and properties of their friend Anna Klecandová-Martenová and her family – or even (partly?) destroyed, thereby depriving us of invaluable documentation. None of Julie Reisserová's personal papers, letters, and manuscripts have been located to date, with the notable exception of the autograph score of the *Pastorale maritimo*, and the signed copies of the three *Esquisses* and *Březen* deposited at the Conservatory of Nancy (France).[5]

---

[1] *Tribuna Popular* (May 26, 1946), 8; *O Jornal* (May 26, 1946), 3; *Le Devoir* (May 3, 1946), 9; see Figure 3. The Reissers had already been in Montreal since October 1945, where Jan was head of the legation of the Provisional International Civil Aviation Organization.

[2] Reisser's mother-in-law (also named Marie Bodláková) accompanied them and died in Rio in 1946; *O Jornal* (November 12, 1946), 2; *Rudé právo* (February 2, 1947), 6.

[3] *Correio da manhã* (March 18, 1949), 2; *Der Bund* (March 18, 1949), 2; *De Volksgazet* (March 18, 1949), 6; *Die Tat* (March 19, 1949), 2; *Neue Zürcher Zeitung* (March 18, 1949), 2; *Oberländer Tagblatt* (March 18, 1949), 2; *O Jornal* (March 18, 1949), 9; *The Civil & Military Gazette* (March 19, 1949), 1; *Telegraf, Baltimore MD* (April 1, 1949), 4. Reisser's career ended officially on February 28, 1949.

[4] From autumn 1938, Jan Reisser and his second wife lived at 102 Primátorská Street (Prague 8). Unless otherwise stated, information about Reisser is drawn from the Archives of the Czech Ministry of Foreign Affairs, Personal files 1945–1992, Box 816, "Reisser, Jan, JURDr."

[5] Some unfindable autographs are mentioned in *Hudební věda*, 4th year (1967), 509.

Figure 1 Julie Reisserová at the Czech Embassy in Copenhagen.
Photography by Holger Damgaard.
Image courtesy of the Royal Danish Library, The Black Diamond; call-number:
Billedsamlingen Udenlandske portrætter. Reisserová, Julie 8vo.

If her premature death put a natural end to her career, Julie Reisserová was silenced a second time by political decisions. Since then, this silence has continued despite a rather detailed obituary jointly written right after her death in 1938 by Josefa Hrdinová and Jiřina Vacková,[6] and the foundation shortly before Christmas 1939 of "The Circle of Friends of Julie Reisserová" ("Kruh přátel Julie Reisserové"). The aim of the latter was to publish and disseminate the musical and poetic works of the artist,[7] the sources of which still remain difficult to access and are practically absent from public libraries.

---

[6] Josefa Hrdinová, "Julie Reisserová: Osobnost a život," *Kulturní letáky. Musea a studijního ústavu odborných škol pro ženská povoláni v Praze* (Prague: Ústav pro učebné pomůcky odborných a průmyslových škol, [1941]), [1]–[2]; Jiřina Vacková "Hudební tvorba Julie Reisserové," in *Kulturní letáky. Musea a studijního ústavu odborných škol pro ženská povoláni v Praze* (Prague: Ústav pro učebné pomůcky odborných a průmyslových škol, [1941]), [2]–[4].

[7] *Národní listy* (January 13, 1940), 3. It is not known how long this circle lasted. See also *Ženská rada*, 16th year, nos. 5–6 (May 31, 1940), 91–92.

The Circle organized concerts around the date of the composer's death, but no scores were printed, not only because of World War II but also because of the passing of Hrdinová, its founder, in 1949.

To celebrate the tenth anniversary of Reisserová's demise (1948), Vacková published the most inestimable source available: *Julie Reisserová: Osobnost a dílo* (*Julie Reisserová: Personality and Work*).[8] As her foreword dated November 1945 indicates, Jan Reisser not only shared information verbally with her but also lent her a large quantity of documents, most of which no longer exist: newspaper clippings, interviews, program notes, photographs, and more importantly his own unpublished memoirs (*Léta s Julkou*), as well as the manuscripts of Julie's collection of poetry (*In margine vitæ*) and scores. She also collected Hrdinová's childhood memories of the composer. Vacková likely began writing her book in 1946, since she refers to the fact that Reisser was then ambassador to Brazil. Yet, this book – the biographical part of which is laconic and based largely on oral testimonies – turns out to be mainly hagiographical, provides virtually no reference to original materials, does not discuss the reception of Reisserová's scores, and offers a rather subjective and descriptive approach to the music. Years later, Vacková gave a controversial lecture on the composer in Prague on March 22, 1957.[9] In 1993, she also released a brief article in *Lidové noviny*, in which she lamented that the fiftieth anniversary of Reisserová's decease had gone unnoticed – in spite of the well-informed entry printed in *Československý hudební slovník osob a institucí* (1965)[10] and her name printed in the *Hudební kalendář a adresář na rok* of 1962[11] – and that the artist had paid unfairly for her husband's political convictions.[12]

Although Czech newspapers scarcely alluded to Reisserová after 1948, she was not entirely forgotten by musicologists and lexicographers. Gracian Černušák considered her as the "first Czech woman composer of importance" in his entry printed in the 1954 edition of the *Grove Dictionary of Music and*

---

[8] Jiřina Vacková, *Julie Reisserová: Osobnost a dílo* (Prague: A. J. Boháč, 1948). In addition, a concert was broadcast on the radio, and two articles were respectively published in *Náš rozhlas* (February 22, 1948), 3 and 14 (concert), and in *Svobodné noviny* (February 29, 1948), 5.

[9] *Literární noviny* (March 16, 1957), 10. According to Vladimír Hloch, some of Vacková's clumsy statements "did her [Reisserová] more harm than good" ("že jí víc ublížila, než prospěla"); Vladimír Hloch's diary, March 22, 1957 ("Důsledky večera Julie Reisserové"), Czech Museum of Music, NM-ČMH č. př. S 27/2000/348. See also Barbora Vacková, "Composers, Women, Mothers, Comrades: The Social Position and Professional Experience of Women Composers in Socialist Czechoslovakia (1948–1989)," unpublished PhD dissertation, University of Huddersfield (2023), 163–164. Hloch was the companion of the prolific composer Sláva Vorlová.

[10] "Reisserová, Julie," in Gracian Černušák, Bohumír Štědroň, and Zdenko Nováček (eds.), *Československý hudební slovník osob a institucí*, 2 vols. (Prague: Státní hudební nakladatelství, 1963–1965), vol. 2, 413.

[11] *Hudební kalendář a adresář na rok* (Prague: SNKLHU, 1962), 23, 32.

[12] Jiřina Vacková, "Ó, božské umění, děkuji ti!", *Lidové noviny* (October 9, 1993), VII.

Musicians,[13] whereas Zdeněk Výborný declared in *Die Musik in Geschichte und Gegenwart* that she "made a great contribution to Czech music" and its dissemination in Western Europe.[14] Her name was also mentioned in passing in a Brazilian article by Marina Moura Peixoto published in September 1957.[15] But Reisserová has since disappeared from all successive printed editions of these two great dictionaries, and she is hardly quoted in recent reference works.[16]

Her name has also been often neglected in most feminist circles since February 26, 1946. On that day, the poet and librettist Vladimír Hloch-Roklan opened the Musical Evening at the Women's Club in Prague – a club founded by Františka Plamínková – with a lecture on Czech women composers, in which he did not fail to cite the three artists born in 1888, Blažena Rylek-Staňková, Hana Králíková-Slavkovská, and Julie Reisserová, whom he stated was the first Czech woman to have written for orchestra.[17]

During the 1930s, the press was unanimous in placing Reisserová, "a figure of international scope,"[18] "in the front rank of modern women composers,"[19] and in recognizing that "she [was] the only woman musician in her country who [had] also earned a well-deserved reputation abroad."[20] Today, her name sometimes appears in scholarly writings, particularly in connection with Roussel, for whom she played a key role in the premiere of his comic opera *Le Testament de la tante Caroline* in 1936. No in-depth study of her activity as composer and

---

[13] Gracian Černušák, "Reisserová, Julie," in George Grove, Eric Blom, and Denis Stevens (eds.), *Grove's Dictionary of Music and Musicians*, 10 vols. (London: MacMillan, St. Martin's Press, 1954), vol. 7, 118. See also *Baker's Biographical Dictionary of Musicians*, 5th ed., rev. Nicolas Slonimsky (New York: G. Schirmer, 1958), 1326.

[14] Zdeněk Výborný, "Reisserová, Julie," in Friedrich Blume (ed.), *Die Musik in Geschichte und Gegenwart: Allgemeine Enzyklopädie der Musik*, 17 vols. (Cassel: Bärenreiter, 1949–1986), vol. 11 (1963), col. 208: "... machte sich um die tschech. Musik verdient."

[15] Marina Moura Peixoto, "A mulher na composição musical (II)," *Diario de noticias: Suplemento Literário* (September 29, 1957), 6.

[16] See in particular, Krešimir Kovačević, Ivona Ajanović-Malinar, and Koraljka Kos (eds.), *Muzička enciklopedija*, 3 vols. (Zagreb: Jugoslavenski leksikografski zavod, 1971–1977), vol. 3, 185; Anna Šerých, "Reisserová [née Kühnlová], Julie," in Julie Anne Sadie and Rhian Samuel (eds.), *The Norton/Grove Dictionary of Women Composers* (New York: W.W. Norton & Co., 1994), 386–387; Christel Nies (ed.), *Entdeckt und aufgeführt. Komponistinnen und ihr Werk IV* (Cassel: Cassel University Press, 2010), 235.

[17] Vladimír Hloch, "Die Entwicklung des weiblichen Tonschaffens in der ČSR" (typescript), Czech Museum of Music, NM-ČMH č. př. 27/2000/348, 13; a handwritten Czech version ("České zeny-skladatelky") is available under the same call number.

[18] Paul Stefan, "Viennese Festival Weeks begin auspiciously," *Musical America* (July 1937), 22.

[19] *Holbæk amts venstreblad* (February 28, 1938), 4: "... stillede hende i forste Række blandt Nutidens kvindelige Komponister."

[20] Gisela Urban, "Komponistin und Diplomatenfrau: Julie Reißerova in Wien," *Neues Wiener Journal* (April 20, 1937), 7: "Ist sie doch die einzige musikschaffende Frau ihres Landes, die sich auch im Ausland einen wohlverdienten Ruf erworben hat." See also *Narod* (October 23, 1931), 3; *Večer* (April 25, 1934), 1.

feminist has been undertaken since that of Vacková, with the exception of my articles and edition of her scores, and Miriam Blümlová's chapter on Czech women composers of the twentieth century.[21] This Element intends to draw up a new biographical sketch of the artist using the many primary sources (such as clippings) neglected by Vacková, the documents reproduced by her but no longer available, as well as recently discovered archives. It also aims to assess Reisserová's views on the status of women composers during the interwar period. To fill in the gaps that remain in the narrative of her life and career, hypotheses are occasionally necessary. The other sections deal with the reception of her six surviving scores, and examine briefly their musical style. This study is complemented by the English translation of the text of the lecture she gave in Vienna in 1937, a catalog of her musical works, and the list of the concerts in which her music was programmed.

2 Biographical Sketch

Little is known about the life of Julie Reisserová, "a hope of Czech music,"[22] for the reasons mentioned in the Introduction. All sources agree that she was a very gifted, intelligent, witty, and likeable person who socialized easily and shone in society, and seems to have enjoyed a rather pleasant and easy existence.

2.1 Origins, Childhood, and Musical Education

Julie Emilie Aloisie Marie Kühnlová [Kühnelová] was born at 14/296 Konviktská Street, in the old Prague parish of Saint Gilles, on October 9, 1888, and was baptized nine days later on October 18.[23] Her father, the official Vojtěch [Adalbert] Kühnl [Kühnel] (1859–1905), was an important figure in the cultural life of the city. Son of the shoemaker Eduard Kühnl [Kühnel] and Magdalena Hölzer, Vojtěch joined the Měšťanská Beseda ("Townpeople's Society") when he was sixteen. The Měšťanská Beseda was founded in Prague in 1845 and consisted of bourgeois, businessmen, civil servants, and intellectuals with a national consciousness. This society was accessible to all classes in the city and to educated people from other states for social entertainment and education.

---

[21] See Select Bibliography, and Miriam Blümlová, "Women Composers in the Czech Lands during the 20th Century," in Elfriede Reissig and Leon Stefanija (eds.), *Composing Women: "Femininity" and Views on Cultures, Gender and Music of Southeastern Europe since 1918* (Vienna: Hollitzer Verlag, 2022), 325–340.

[22] P. Stf., "Julie Reisserova gestorben," *Die Stunde* (March 3, 1938), [3]: "eine Hoffnung der tschechischen Musik."

[23] Birth register, Kostel sv. Jiljí (Church of Saint-Gilles), Prague City Archives, JIL N21 [1886–1893], fol. 113v–114r (116v–117r). See also police records, National Archives of the Czech Republic, Police Directorate I, conscription (1850–1914), box 263, fol. 618r. The old building on Konviktská Street no longer exists.

During the 1850s, this type of association emerged in various cities as a reaction of the Czech-speaking population to the activities of similar cultural associations of German-speaking fellow citizens. Vojtěch Kühnl became a member of the Entertainment Committee in 1876, and eventually served as its chairman for ten years, before resigning in early 1890. He also served on its Administrative Committee from 1880. Then in 1901, he was appointed deputy mayor by a special vote of the members. His directorship of the Entertainment Committee was very successful and increased the society's membership.[24]

Julie's mother, Marie Majdalena Neander (born in 1862), came from an old and wealthy family of Prague merchants, who owned the house "U mouřenína" at the corner of Mostecká (5/282) and Lazenská Streets in Malá Strana. She was the daughter of Antonín Neander and of Emilie Kleinberg who was related to several noble families. While Vojtěch Kühnl was an optimistic and cheerful man with a warm nature, an excellent musician, and lover of music, Marie Majdalena was a gentle and peaceful woman who loved classical literature and who played the piano superbly.

Vojtěch Karel Antonín, Julie's older brother, was born on April 30, 1886. He married Barbara Bendová on April 10, 1918, in Prague, and died in Potštejn (district of Rychnov nad Kněžnou) on February 9, 1942.[25] He worked as an engineer, but distinguished himself above all for having translated the libretto of Wagner's *Siegfried* into Czech for the first series of performances of the opera at the Brno National Theater in April and June 1931.[26]

Coming from a Catholic family of high social rank, the two children benefited from a thorough intellectual and musical education. Vojtěch studied piano with Karel Slavkovský, a pupil of Smetana and a friend of Dvořák, who had founded a piano school in the early 1870s. Vojtěch was assiduous in practicing his instrument, and frequently asked his more gifted sister to play the piano with him. During their school years, both organized concerts at home that were attended by their cousins, classmates, and students. During these youthful events Julie took up the habit of improvising freely at the piano, which prompted her parents to send her to the Dvořákeum. The Dvořákeum was a private musical institution established in Prague around 1904–1906 by the organist and conductor Eduard Tregler and Antonín Herman. It was there that she received her first music lessons with Václav Talich (five years her senior),

---

[24] *Národní listy* (July 7, 1905), 3 (obituary of Vojtěch Kühnl); František v. Schwarz, *Památník Besedy Měšťanské v Praze na oslavu padesátileté činnosti spolku 1845–6–1895–6* (Prague: Měšťanské Besedy v Praze, 1896), 107, 141, and 152.

[25] Birth register, Kostel sv. Jiljí (Church of Saint-Gilles), Prague City Archives, JIL N20 [1880–1886], fol. 288v–289r (290v–291r).

[26] Richard Wagner, *Siegfried*, translated by Vojtěch Kühnel (Prague: B. M. Klika, 1931).

between 1906 and 1908, that is, between the return of Talich from Tbilisi and his stay in Ljubljana. (We do not know the content of these lessons.) It is, however, very likely that young Julie was introduced to the basics of music at a much earlier age, as it is hard to believe that she practiced the keyboard at an early stage without a minimum of instruction: Was she taught by Slavkovský at the same time as her brother? Then, she studied piano with Adolf Mikeš at his own school founded in 1903, and prepared for the state examination under his guidance. From about 1914 she trained as a dramatic soprano with the tenor Richard Figar (Fikar, alias Hofer) at the singing school he had opened in Prague in 1908. Because Figar had held the title roles of Tannhäuser, Lohengrin, and that of Walther von Stolzing (*The Master Singers of Nuremberg*) in particular, she focused chiefly on Wagnerian characters, but she had to abandon the idea to become an opera singer due to vocal overexertion. This made her decide to pursue her deepest dream: to become a composer. Josef Bohuslav Foerster accepted her as a private composition student in 1919. He taught her harmony, counterpoint, and musical forms. In his memoirs, he acknowledges that Julie Kühnlová was one of his best and most diligent pupils: her music evidenced originality, intelligence, and immense sensitivity.[27] Foerster's lessons lasted until Julie's marriage in 1921. In the end, Julie never attended the Prague Conservatory, but took only private lessons to master the arcana of music.[28]

Almost nothing is known about her general instruction. At nine years old, she is said to have been lively and very gifted. She enjoyed learning in a playful way, and only what interested her. Her grades were excellent.[29] It can be surmised that she was first educated privately or in one of the city's institutions for young women. Then, as a teenager, she attended high school. Shortly after her father's death, she studied languages at Charles University, which enabled her to eventually teach English and French, and to be financially independent. Around 1911,[30] she frequented the Hudební klub (Music Club) which was firmly linked to Charles University. This circle of intellectuals, active from 1911 to 1927, was founded by the musicologist and Smetana scholar Zdeněk Nejedlý, who would later become the first Minister of Culture and Education of the Czechoslovak Socialist Republic, and his university students and listeners. One purpose of the Club was to promote Smetana's Czech identity as opposed to the Lisztian and Wagnerian image, constructed by members of the Umělecká Beseda ("Artistic Society") founded in January 1863 by Bedřich Smetana,

---

[27] Foerster's memoirs quoted from Vacková, *Julie Reisserová*, 8–9.
[28] The name of Julie Kühnlová never appears in the archives of the Prague Conservatory.
[29] Hrdinová, "Julie Reisserová," [1].
[30] In 1909 according to Vacková, *Julie Reisserová*, 7. This date is obviously incorrect, as the Club had not yet been founded at that time.

Foerster, and Josef Mánes, among several leading artists, to give Czech culture an European dimension that was lacking at the time.[31] Another was to attend scholarly lectures, to see dramatic performances, and to discuss contemporary music, mainly that of Wagner and Mahler. The Club proved to be of the utmost importance in Julie's life. There, she met – among others – the scholar Vladimír Helfert, the composer and conductor Karel Boleslav Jirák, and above all, Jan Reisser, three years her junior and a student of Nejedlý at Charles University.

Jan Václav Reisser was born in the parish of the Church of the Holy Spirit (Staré Město) on September 12, 1891, and was baptized twelve days later on September 24.[32] His father, Jan Reisser [II], was employed by the Czech Post Office in Prague, first as secretary, and then from January 1902 as chief commissioner assigned to the Inspection Service.[33] His grandfather, Jan Reisser [I], was guard inspector at the Prague penitentiary.[34] His mother, Anna, née Hedviková, was the daughter of the master of mines Jan Hedvik. Like Julie, he benefited from the music lessons of Mikeš and Figar, as well as from Bohumila Rosenkrancová and Albín Ším. While studying law at Charles University, he participated in the creation of the Music Club to which he contributed several articles on Smetana. He subsequently wrote a handful of papers on various composers (notably Ravel and Roussel), and essays on opera, such as the polemical pamphlet *The Singing Culture of Our Theater*.[35] He even collected some of Smetana's writings in a book published in 1920.[36] He earned his doctorate in law from Charles University in November 1915, and entered the diplomatic service four years later in December 1919.

2.2 A Life Abroad

Julie Kühnlová married Jan Reisser on December 15, 1921.[37] Shortly afterward, the couple moved to Geneva for a few months, where Jan Reisser had been appointed on October 4, 1921, as secretary of the Czechoslovak Embassy to the

---

[31] Kelly St. Pierre, "Smetana's 'Vyšehrad' and Mythologies of Czechness in Scholarship," *19th-Century Music*, 37 (Fall 2013), 110–111; Benjamin Curtis, *Music Makes the Nation: Nationalist Composers and Nation Building in Nineteenth-Century Europe* (Amherst NY: Cambria Press, 2008), 64; Petr Čornej, *Historici, historiografie a dějepis: Studie, črty, eseje* (Prague: Univerzita Karlova v Praze, 2016), "Hudební klub v Praze (1911–1927)," 266–319 (on Julie Kühnlová, see 289, 298).

[32] Birth register, Kostel sv. Ducha (Church of the Holy Spirit), Prague City Archives, DUCH N14 [1887–1892], fol. 319v–320r. He was born at 22/866 Dušní Street.

[33] *Katolické listy*, 332 (December 3, 1898), 4; *Katolické listy*, 358 (December 31, 1901), 4.

[34] *Čech*, vol. 21, no. 219 (1889), 1.

[35] "Reisser, Jan," in Černušák *et al.* (eds.), *Československý hudební*, vol. 2, 413; Jan Reisser, *Pěvecká kultura našeho divadla* (Prague: B. Kočí, 1918).

[36] Jan Reisser (ed.), *Bedřich Smetana: Články a referáty, 1862–1865* (Prague: Česká grafická unie, 1920).

[37] No trace of this marriage has been found in the Prague parish registers.

League of Nations, and to Bern on March 30, 1922, where he held the position of counselor to the Czechoslovak legation.[38] During their stay in Switzerland between 1921 and 1929, Reisserová was able to perfect her musical training. Thus, in 1923–1924, she deepened her harmonic knowledge and Germanic instrumentation by analyzing neoromantic scores – such as those by Ludwig Thuille – under the guidance of Ernst Hohlfeld, a former pupil of Hans Pfitzner and then the Kapellmeister of the Bern Stadttheater.[39] She once stated that while in Bern she had the opportunity to conduct a choir and an orchestra:[40] Did Hohlfeld give her additional training in this art? According to the obituary published in the Swiss newspaper *Der Bund*, she also benefited from the lessons of an obscure Bernese music pedagogue named Spenzer, but no other source corroborates this information.[41] In any case, it was at Bern that she overcame – at thirty-five-years old – her doubts about her abilities to compose seriously, and penned three of the four songs of the cycle *Březen*, the orchestral piece *La Bise*, and *Allégresse* that was to become the third movement of the *Esquisses* for piano. It was also from 1927 onward that her music began to be performed in public, and her fame to grow all over Europe. How she managed to gain access to the stage is unknown; perhaps Jan Reisser and his acquaintances at the embassy played a role in this.[42] He and his wife were indeed often invited to official dinners, such as the one given by Jean Hennessy, French ambassador in Bern, on December 22, 1927.[43]

By the turn of 1924–1925, Reisserová went to Paris to seek advice from Albert Roussel. While she received her first musical education through family connections, she may have discovered Roussel's music in December 1920 when his First Symphony was played by the Czech Philharmonic Orchestra directed by Václav Talich, and ten months later at a concert under the auspices of the French Minister of Foreign Affairs Aristide Briand, in which the orchestra gave *Le Festin de l'araignée* conducted by René-Emmanuel Baton.[44] She submitted

---

[38] *Národní politika* (March 14, 1922), 5. Jan Reisser had been named consul on February 12, 1921; see *Národní politika* (February 19, 1921), 6. See also Jindřich Dejmek, František Kolář (eds.), *Dokumenty československé zahraniční politika: Československá zahraniční politika a vznik Malé dohody, 1920–1921*, 2 vols. (Prague: Karolinum, 2004), vol. 2, 575.

[39] Hohlfeld may also have helped her to have Smetana's *The Bartered Bride* staged at the Bern Stadttheater in 1923; see *Večer* (April 25, 1934), 1.

[40] Vilém Závada, "Skladatelka Julie Reisserová o sobě," *Rozpravy Aventina*, vol. 7, no. 6 (5 October 1931), 44; Josefa Hrdinová, "Julie Reisserová," *Škola a rodina*, 5th year, year 1931–1932 (December 1931), 49; *Neues Wiener Journal* (April 20, 1937), 7.

[41] W. R. B., "Julia Reißerova," *Der Bund* (March 17, 1938), 3.

[42] Reisser was indeed accused of having been mainly concerned by costly social events during his stay in Geneva. See Miroslav Brejcha, "Československý Diplomat JUDr. Robert Flieder," unpublished PhD dissertation, Charles University (2006), 39.

[43] *Le Gaulois* (December 28, 1927), 2.

[44] Aleš Březina, "Albert Roussel a jeho česká přátelství," *Harmonie* (August 2017), 4.

to Roussel *La Bise* and a now lost piano piece whose thematic content was reused in the first movement of the *Suita*. The French composer perused them,[45] and concluded that they were "very fresh." Reisserová would have answered that she was of the opinion that "music should follow the beats of the heart," to which Roussel would have replied: "Then your heart beats very irregularly."[46] Roussel, who seldom accepted private students, agreed to instruct her in rigorous contrapuntal writing, and the subtlety, richness, and colors of French orchestration. She began with four-voice harmonization of chorales and counterpoint exercises. All in all, the French master gave her 241 lessons between January 18, 1925, and February 20, 1937, but only ten or so to Bohuslav Martinů.[47] In the lecture she gave in Vienna, Reisserová said that she had studied with Roussel for only five years and that he had stopped teaching her after the first performance of one of her orchestral works in Paris (i.e., *La Bise* on April 23, 1929). Would this suggest that she had in fact studied with him for only four years and that they met informally afterward?[48] Her lessons with Roussel marked a long-lasting and sincere friendship that made her travel back and forth between her home and Paris, and a friendship that ended with the death of her mentor.[49] The latter appreciated her as a composer and as a person, and it was "irresistible for everyone when he slowly pronounce[d] her first name in Czech: Ju-lin-ka."[50] Reisserová was often invited to visit Le Vasterival, Roussel's house at Varengeville-sur-Mer (Normandy), where she notably composed her *Pastorale maritimo* dedicated to Roussel's wife, Blanche Preisach.[51] She also spontaneously translated into Czech the libretto of his *opéra bouffe*, *Le Testament de la tante Caroline*, for its creation at the opera house in Olomouc on November 14, 1936.[52] (This suggests that she probably had good contacts with Adolf Heller, then director of the Olomouc institution.)

---

[45] Based on Reisserová's talk in Vienna (Appendix A), she played him a piano piece but did not provide further detail.
[46] Dialogue quoted from Vacková, *Julie Reisserová*, 12.
[47] According to Roussel's diaries. Acknowledgments are due to Damien Top who shared this information with me.
[48] Jelena Holečková-Heidenreichová, "Za Julií Reisserovou," *Ženská rada*, 14th year, no. 4 (April 1938), 80, also states that Reisserová studied with Roussel for only four years.
[49] It seems that Roussel sent her a last letter, now lost, on July 30 or 31, 1937.
[50] J. M. Pellé, "Julie Reisserová v Paříži," *Národní sjednocení* (February 12, 1937), 5: "pro všechny neodolatelné, když vyslovuje po česku pomalu její příjmení: Ju-lin-ka."
[51] In 1925, Reisserová, Roussel, and his wife were photographed at the front door of the house: Nicole Labelle (ed.), *Albert Roussel: Lettres et écrits* (Paris: Flammarion, 1987), IV (plates). On Roussel, see Damien Top, *Albert Roussel* (Paris: Bleu nuit éditeur, 2016). Julie and Jan Reisser usually stayed at the Hôtel de la Terrasse.
[52] *Le Figaro* (January 21, 1937), 5; B., "Tchécoslovaquie," *La Revue musicale*, vol. 17, no. 170 (December 1936), 454; Miriam Hasíková [Blümlová], *Meziválečné hudební divadlo v Olomouci* (Olomouc: Univerzita Palackého v Olomouci, 2016), 224–230. Roussel's score is dedicated to "Jan et Julie Reisser."

In an autobiographical record – a questionnaire ("Dotazník") sent to Reisserová in 1931 by the editors of the music dictionary *Pazdírkův Hudební slovník naučný* – she claimed to have attended "Lily" (*recte* Nadia) Boulanger's classes at the École Normale de Musique without giving any further detail.[53] (Boulanger and the Czech artist were perhaps not on particularly good terms, since the latter got Boulanger's first name wrong, and never mentioned her studies at the École Normale in interviews.) Reisserová may have also frequented the Schola Cantorum irregularly, because she alluded to Vincent d'Indy and one of their discussions in the lecture she delivered in Vienna. In any case, she was evidently acquainted with many artists, musicians, and intellectuals while in Paris. In 1927 alone, the year of her first documented public concerts, she had the good fortune to benefit from a cycle of evenings dedicated to the promotion of Czech composers. Thus, she ran into Julien Tiersot at the "Festival of Czechoslovak music" ("Festival de musique Tchécoslovaque") hosted by Alexandre Mercereau at his home (241, Boulevard Raspail) on February 24,[54] and Jane Mortier who accompanied Jeanne Bathori and Zdeňka Krausová in three of her songs (two of which were probably excerpted from *Březen*)[55] at the March concerts given successively at La Sorbonne, and at the Salle Pleyel. Besides, she opened her mind to new trends, such as French impressionism and the ballets of Stravinsky under whose influence she composed *Jaro v ulici*. All in all, Paris remained a place where the Reissers often visited and sojourned between 1924 and 1937.[56]

After leaving Switzerland in 1929, the couple lived one year in Prague, before settling in Belgrade, where Jan Reisser was assigned as head of the Czechoslovak legation on August 25, 1930 (he was transferred there on December 1, 1930). As an official member of the legation, Julie Reisserová organized, or took part in the organization of many musical events in which Czech composers, such as Martinů and herself, were at the forefront. Thus, pieces by the two composers – along with ones by Foerster, Novák, Suk, and Janáček, to name but a few – were performed on

---

[53] "Dotazník," in "Reisserová" folder, Center for Music Lexicography in Brno, no call-number, [1]. Oldřich Pazdírek, Vladimír Helfert, and Gracian Černušák (eds.), *Pazdírkův hudební slovník naučný* (Brno: Oldřich Pazdírek, 1937–1940). See also Černušák *et al.* (eds.), *Československý hudební*, vol. 2, 413.
[54] *La Semaine à Paris* (February 18–25, 1927), 41; *Národní listy* (March 31, 1927), 9; *Sveta Cecilija*, vol. 21 no. 4 (July 1927), 193.
[55] Závada, "Skladatelka Julie Reisserová o sobě," 44. In this interview, Reisserová mentioned "Dvě melodie": it is likely that the phrase refers to *Světlo*, *Nostalgie*, and/or *Za svítání*, three songs that were often sung that year. *La Semaine à Paris* (March 4–11, 1927), 36, provides the same titles in French: "2 mélodies" (followed by "1re audition").
[56] As Martinů wrote in a letter dated May 26, 1932: Gabriela Všetičková and Jaromír Synek (eds.), *Drazí II: Dopisy Bohuslava Martinů rodině v Poličce z let 1932 a 1933 – Dear All II: Bohuslav Martinů's Letters to His Family in Poličce in 1932 and 1933* (Olomouc: Univerzita Palackého v Olomouci, 2019), 152.

April 23, 1932, during a concert of Czech modern music attended by members of the Czechoslovak diplomatic corps and notables of Belgrade.[57] A year later, Reisserová's *Pastorale maritimo* was premiered there by the Philharmonic Orchestra.[58] In Serbia, she met the well-known piano teacher and director of the Stanković Musical School, Emil Hájek, who prepared the vocal score of *Březen*, and played the three *Esquisses* many times.[59] Unfortunately, the Reissers' desire to arrange a concert of Roussel's music under the auspices of the Embassy met with the disapproval of Ambassador Robert Flieder and his wife. Although the two couples had known each other since Bern, personal relations deteriorated in February and March 1933, leading to a reshuffle of the legation.[60] As the Reissers had quickly become the center of Belgrade's intellectual, literary, and artistic microcosm, a group of friends, writers, musicians, painters, sculptors, and actors planned a farewell banquet on the following September 23, just after the world premiere of the *Pastorale maritimo*.[61] Among these artists, Vladimír Žedrinsky, the set dresser, painter, and contributor to the *Politika* newspaper, should be singled out for his caricature drawing of Julie's portrait.[62]

Between October 1, 1933, and August 31, 1936, the Reissers were in Copenhagen.[63] The stay in Denmark was particularly fruitful, since it was there that Reisserová had the occasion to publish some of her scores and to forge a reputation as a musician during parties held at various Embassies.[64] Thus, she was able to rub shoulders with ministers and other political figures at social dinners, and to have her works sung there. One of the most important cultural events that took place in Copenhagen during Jan and Julie Reisser's residency was undoubtedly the "Czech month in Denmark," which included book and painting exhibitions, as well as concerts. Jan Reisser and the Danish Minister of Trade and Industry, Christen Nielsen Hauge, launched this "month" – which lasted until March 7 – at the Museum of Art and Industry on February 10, 1934.

---

[57] *Politika* (April 25, 1932), 6; *Národní listy večerník*, vol. 72, no. 118 (April 28, 1932), 2.

[58] It is at least what can be guessed from J. H. H. [Julius Heidenreich], "Za Julií Reisserovou," *Československo-jihoslovanská revue*, vol. 8, nos. 3–4 (1938), 94.

[59] Heidenreich, "Za Julií Reisserovou," 94.

[60] Brejcha, "Československy Diplomat JUDr. Robert Flieder," 50 (the Flieders considered they should only promote Czech artists); *Národní politika* (May 2, 1933), 2.

[61] *Politika* (September 21, 1933), 4.

[62] The portrait, dated 1933, is reproduced in *Zvuk* (May 7, 1933), 263, and *Večer* (April 25, 1934), 1.

[63] *Bulletin périodique de la presse yougoslave du 27 juillet au 30 septembre 1933*, 109 (October 16–18, 1933), 9. Reisser was appointed to Denmark on September 6, 1933, and was notified of his new position at the Foreign Ministry on July 7, 1936.

[64] By 1936, Reisserová was sufficiently renowned to be included among the members of the Association for the Protection of Czech Authors, Composers, Writers and Music Publishers (Ochranné Sdruzeni Autorské Csl. Skladatelù Spisovatelù a Nakladatelu Hudebnich), which had agreements with the American Society of Composers, Authors, and Publishers; see *List of Members of the American Society of Composers, Authors, and Publishers and Similar Foreign Societies as of January 1st, 1936* ([New York]: ASCAP, [1936]), R–6.

According to various press clippings, it was on the same February 10 at the Koncertpalaet that Julie Reisserová's name first appeared to the Copenhagen public: the French opera singer Alice Raveau sang *À l'Aube* (*Za svítání*), which was enthusiastically received by the audience and the Czech and Danish authorities.[65] Seven days later,

> S. Exc. le ministre de France en Danemark et Mme Manceron ont donné une grande soirée au cours de laquelle s'est fait entendre la cantatrice Alice Raveau, qui a interprété, entre autres, des airs d'*Orphée* de Gluck; quelques morceaux de compositeurs français modernes et *À l'Aube*, œuvre d'une jeune compositrice, Mme Reisserova, élève de Roussel et femme du chargé d'affaires de Tchécoslovaquie à Copenhague.[66]

> His Excellency the Minister of France in Denmark [Charles-Arsène Henry] and Mrs. Manceron gave a great evening [at the French Embassy] during which the opera singer Alice Raveau was heard, who interpreted, among other things, airs from *Orphée* by Gluck; a few pieces by modern French composers and *À l'Aube* a work by a young composer, Mrs. Reisserová, a student of Roussel and wife of the Czechoslovakian *chargé d'affaires* in Copenhagen.

That the columnist used the phrase "young composer" confirms that Reisserová's reputation was not yet well established outside a small circle of musicians, even though *Březen* and the *Suita* had already met with great success in Prague in October 1931. On March 2, Danish soprano Inger Raasløff gave a recital accompanied on the piano by Christian Christiansen, in which she performed several Czech folk songs, as well as *Za svítání* and *Světlo* (from *Březen*). On the same evening, the Danish Radio broadcast a recital by Emil Hájek, who played Reisserová's *Allégresse* as well as pieces by other Czech composers. The highlight of the month was the gala evening organized by the Danish-Czechoslovak Society at the Hornung & Møller Concert Hall. Jan Reisser opened the evening with a lecture on modern Czech music, followed by a concert. Hájek played piano pieces by Czech composers old and new, while soprano Else Schøtt sang pieces by Smetana and Dvořák, and "clearly shaped and sonically beautiful compositions" by Reisserová, the hostess of the event.[67] Finally, a second gala evening took place on March 7, offered by the "All People Association," in the course of

---

[65] Else Moltke, "Český měsíc v Dánsku," *Národní listy* (April 18, 1934), 4; *Národní politika* (March 6, 1934), 7; *Národní politika* (March 16, 1934), 3.

[66] *Comœdia* (February 19, 1934), 4. See also *Comœdia* (February 18, 1934), 2; *Le Temps* (February 18, 1934), 1; *Le Figaro* (February 17, 1934), 3.

[67] *Národní listy* (April 18, 1934), 4: "jasně formované a zvukově krásné skladby." See also *Národní politika* (March 6, 1934), 7; *Prager Presse* (March 13, 1934), 3 (photograph of Julie and Jan Reisser).

which Jan Reisser paid tribute to President Masaryk and Hájek played, among others, the first of the three *Esquisses*.

At the margins of this "Czech month," the social life of the Reissers was particularly rich, and left traces in the press. Thus, it is known that late in April or early in May 1935, they were invited to attend a lunch offered by the French *chargé d'affaires* in Denmark, Paul Petit, where they met the USSR Minister Nikolai Tikhmeneff.[68] Conversely, the Reissers also loved to receive Danish and visiting foreign musicians in the villa of the Czechoslovakian Embassy. The obituaries printed in Danish newspapers after Reisserová's death unanimously praised her for being a radiant and hospitable hostess and for the warmth with which she and her husband had received visitors.[69] The couple indeed took care of all the artists who passed through the capital where they lived, building contacts and organizing receptions and concerts for them: "In Copenhagen, as elsewhere, the home of Dr. Jan Reisser and his wife has become a gathering place for everything to do with art."[70] In that respect, conductor Jaroslav Krombholc later recalled that for his concert tour in Brazil in 1947, Reisser "took care of the matter and in conjunction with our authorities," so that the tour "became an official venture to promote our [Czech] music."[71] In February 1936, Reisserová managed to have Roussel invited to Copenhagen where his Third Symphony and his Sinfonietta were given by the Denmark Radio Symphony Orchestra under the baton of Nikolai Malko.[72] Wherever they were, the Reissers indeed succeeded in promoting the culture of their native country and more generally contemporary European music, sometimes contributing reviews of musical events to various newspapers and magazines, such as *České slovo, Lod, Moderní revue, Právo Lidu, Přítomnost, Tempo, Zvuk*, or *Revue de Genève*.[73]

Reisserová's growing reputation as a composer obviously led to her music being increasingly programmed by renowned artists and broadcast on various European national radio stations, including in Latvia, Finland, Sweden, and Romania. The countries where her music was heard most often between 1927 and 1941 were

---

[68] *L'Européen* (May 3, 1935), 9. According to Martinů, the Reissers spent a few days in Polička in February 1935; see Gabriela Coufalová Vít Zouhar (ed.), *Dear Miloš: Bohuslav Martinů's Letters to Miloš Šafránek* (Olomouc: Univerzita Palackého v Olomouci, 2019), 70.

[69] *Berlingske tidende* (February 27, 1938), 5; *Nationaltidende* (February 27, 1938), 2.

[70] Ursus, "Julie Reisserova," *Forum* (February 29, 1936), 19: "I København som andre Steder er Dr. Jan Reisser og hans Frues Hjem blevet et Samlingssted for alt, hvad der har med Kunst at gøre."

[71] Quoted from Martin Kučera, *Drama dirigenta: Jaroslav Krombholc v osidlech doby* (Prague: Univerzita Karlova, 2018), 115: "ujal se věci a ve spojení s našimi úřady stal se můj zájezd vlastně oficiálním podnikem s cílem propagovat naši hudbu." See also *O Cruzeiro: Revista* (September 27, 1947), 82.

[72] Knudaage Riisager, "Danemark," *La Revue musicale*, vol. 17, no. 163 (February 1936), 144.

[73] Vacková, *Julie Reisserová*, 9; Černušák *et al.* (eds.), *Československý hudební*, vol. 2, 413; *Le Gaulois* (March 30, 1924), 6. Reisserová's report of the Olomouc premiere of *Le Testament de la tante Caroline* was printed in *Tempo* (December 3, 1936), 63.

Julie Reisserová (1888–1938) 15

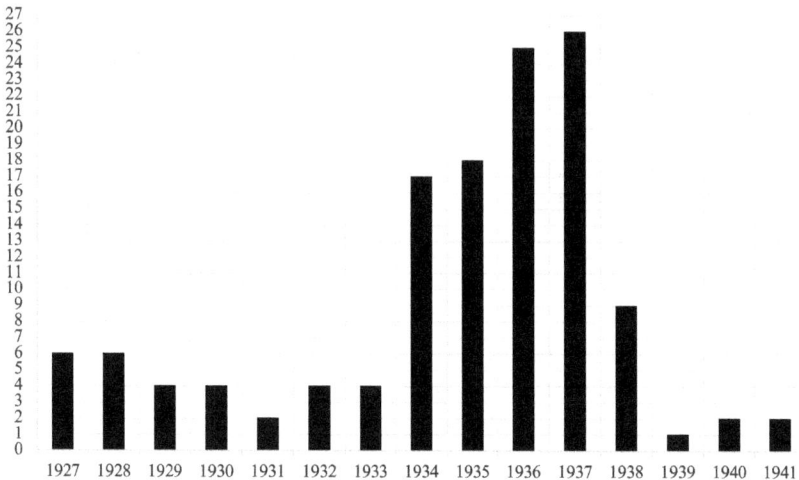

Figure 2 Documented number of public and radio performances per year between 1927 and 1941 (Appendix C). Newspapers and magazines allude to other performances without providing usable data.

Czechoslovakia (34 known concerts), Denmark (34), France (25), and Switzerland (13).[74] Interestingly enough, no concert of her music was recorded in Italy, Spain, or England, where Jan Reisser was never on duty. As shown in Figure 2, the years 1934–1937 were the most successful in terms of number of public performances, which is partly explained by the publication of *Březen* and the *Esquisses* in Copenhagen. Hence, between 1927 and 1941 the songs of *Březen* – either in their symphonic or piano version – were very popular (around fifty-nine performances of *Světlo*, forty-nine of *Za svítání*, and thirty-nine of *Nostalgie* and *Jaro v ulici*); *Esquisses* no. 1 and 2 were played in public twenty-six and twenty-two times respectively, and *Allégresse* (*Esquisses* no. 3) thirty-three times. The *Pastorale maritimo* and *La Bise* (*Suita* no. 3) remained far behind with eighteen (perhaps even more) and fourteen performances respectively.

The festival accompanying the International Congress of Music Composers, organized in Vichy from September 2 to 9, 1935, accelerated Reisserová's career as an international composer. Under the presidency of Richard Strauss and vice-presidency of Albert Roussel, this congress brought together a large number of French and foreign composers.[75] It was at the bandstand of the Parc

---

[74] For a list of these concerts, see Vacková, *Julie Reisserová*, 53–57; Jean-Paul C. Montagnier, "Autour de la *Pastorale maritimo* de Julie Reisserová (1888–1938)," *Revue belge de musicologie*, LXXIV (2020),160–163; and Appendix C.

[75] Paul Bertand, "Le Mouvement musical en Province," *Le Ménestrel*, 97th year, nos. 37–38 (September 13 and 20, 1935), 286; Henry Prunières, "Le festival du conseil permanent pour la coopération internationale des compositeurs de musique à Vichy," *La Revue musicale*, vol. 16, no. 159 (September–October 1935), 229–232.

des Sources, a stone's throw from the Palais des Congrès, that the *Pastorale maritimo*, conducted by Louis Fourestier, aroused the interest of the journalists and musicians present, such as Darius Milhaud who classified the Czech artist among the authors of "good music."[76] Gustave Samazeuilh did not take the trouble to list the names of all the composers played each afternoon at this bandstand but did mention "Mrs. Reisserová (whose delicate *pastorale* represented the Czechoslovak school)."[77] It is undoubtedly in Vichy that she first met the director of the Nancy Conservatory, Alfred Bachelet, to whom we owe the conservation of the autograph manuscript and the photostatic edition of the score.[78] The *Pastorale maritimo* quickly became the most often played and/or broadcast orchestral work of the composer, and lastingly remained in the memories of musicians: in 1960, René Dumesnil still considered this piece to be one the most representative of Czech music of the first half of the twentieth century, along with works by František Bartoš.[79]

Appointed head of the Transport Department of the Ministry of Foreign Affairs on September 1, 1936,[80] Jan Reisser and his wife returned to their apartment in Prague (33/378 Podskalská Street; Nové Mesto), which would be their base until the composer's death. In 1937, they spent some time in Paris and Brussels. On January 20 that year, Jan Reisser – likely accompanied by his wife – and a large number of politicians and personalities attended the lunch hosted by Marcel-Henri Jaspar, the Belgian Minister of Transport in his ministry in Brussels on the occasion of the Belgian-Czech aeronautical conference.[81] Eight days later, Reisserová was present at the Salle Pleyel for the Paris premiere of the *Pastorale maritimo* under the baton of Charles Munch (Figure 5), before returning to Brussels on March 17, where she was invited by Aline van Bärentzen:

> Mme Aline Van Barentzen a offert, en son hôtel avenue de Tervueren, une soirée de musique tchéco-slovaque à laquelle assistèrent de nombreux auditeurs, parmi lesquels on notait S. E. M. Slavik, ministre de Tchécoslovaquie, et d'autres personnalités du monde diplomatique: MM. J. Jongen, A. de Greef, J. Van Straelen; Mmes Ed. Deru, J. Rogatchewsky, S. Huysmans,

---

[76] Darius Milhaud, "Le Festival de Vichy," *Le Jour* (September 10, 1935), 6: "bonne musique."
[77] Gustave Samazeuilh, "Le Festival international de Vichy," *La Revue hebdomadaire*, 44th year, vol. IX (September 1935), 495: "Mme Reisserova (dont une délicate pastorale représentait l'école tchécoslovaque)." Paul Le Flem provided a list of the scores performed during the festival in *Comœdia* (September 12, 1935), 1–2. Another list is available in *Hufvudstadsbladet* (September 3, 1935), 6. See also Montagnier, "Autour de la *Pastorale maritimo*," 143–166.
[78] A month after the congress, Reisserová sent Bachelet a signed copy of *Březen*: "À maître A. Bachelet/bien sincèrement/[signature] Julie Reisserové/Varengeville Plage/i octobre 1935." Library of the Conservatoire régional du Grand-Nancy, call-number YREI 002.
[79] Jules Combarieu and René Dumesnil, *Histoire de la musique des origines à nos jours*, [new ed.], 5 vols., vol. 5: *La première moitié du XXe siècle par René Dumesnil* (Paris: Armand Colin, 1960), 341.
[80] *Národní politika* (September 22, 1936), 9. [81] *L'Indépendance belge* (January 21, 1937), 10.

etc., etc. Le programme, fort applaudi, comprenait le Trio de V. Novak, des pièces de piano de Suk, Jirak, Martinu, des mélodies de Novak, Vomacka et Jirak, un duo pour violon et violoncelle de Martinu et, en première audition, des œuvres de Mme Julia Reisserova. Les exécutants étaient l'hôtesse elle-même, l'excellente pianiste Mme Van Barentzen, Mme Reisserova dans la partie pianistique de ses œuvres, Mlle Arvez-Vernet, de l'Opéra, cantatrice; MM. Brunschwig, violoniste, Huvelin, violoncelliste, M. de Bourguignon au clavier d'accompagnement.[82]

Mrs. Aline Van Bärentzen offered, in her mansion on the Avenue de Tervueren, an evening of Czech-Slovak music, which was attended by numerous auditors, among whom were H. E. Slavík, Minister of Czechoslovakia, and other personalities from the diplomatic [and artistic] world: Messrs. J[oseph]. Jongen, A[rthur]. de Greef, J[an]. Van Straelen; Mrs. Ed[ouard]. Deru, J[oseph]. Rogatchewsky, S[ara]. Huysmans, etc., etc. The program, which was well received, included the Trio by V[ítězslav]. Novák, piano pieces by [Josef] Suk, [Karel Bohuslav] Jirák, [Bohuslav] Martinů, songs by Novák, [Boleslav] Vomáčka and Jirák, a duet for violin and cello by Martinů and, as a first performance, works by Mrs. Julia Reisserová. The performers were the hostess herself, the excellent pianist Mrs. Van Bärentzen, Mrs. Reisserová in the piano part of her works, Ms. [Gilberte] Arvez-Vernet, from the Opera, singer; Messrs. [Dany] Brunschwig, violinist, [André] Huvelin, cellist, Mr. [Francis] de Bourguignon at the accompanying keyboard.

Finally, she was in Dieppe – along with Jacques Ibert, Arthur Honegger, Roland-Manuel, and René Dumesnil – for the funeral of Albert Roussel on August 27, 1937.[83]

2.3 Death and Aftermath

In 1937 (or a little earlier?), Julie Reisserová was struck down by an insidious and incurable ailment whose nature is not documented. She ultimately had to undergo surgery, which took place around February 10, 1938 at the Podolsk Sanatorium in Prague (Pražské Sanatorium v Podoli). Unable to recover, Julie Reisserová passed away there on the afternoon of Friday February 25, 1938. The news spread abroad quickly relayed by the main national newspapers.[84]

---

[82] *L'Indépendance belge* (March 22, 1937), 6; *Lidové noviny* (March 24, 1937), 9. During this event, the song cycle *Pod sněhem* received its "first performance" outside Czechoslovakia.
[83] *L'Action française* (August 28, 1937), 2; *Excelsior* (August 28, 1937), 7.
[84] *Moravská orlice* (February 26, 1938), 3; *Národní listy* (February 26, 1938), 3; *Národní politika* (February 26, 1938), 1; *Prager Presse* (February 26, 1938), 5; *Venkov* (February 26, 1938), 4; *Berlingste Tidende* (February 27, 1938), 5; *Nationaltidende* (February 27, 1938), 2; *Holbæk amts venstreblad* (February 28, 1938), 4; *Journal du Jura* (February 28, 1938), [8]; *Hufvudstadsbladet* (March 1, 1938), 8; *Feuille d'avis de Neuchatel* (March 2, 1938), 6; *Journal de Genève* (March 2, 1938), 2; *Die Stunde* (March 3, 1938), 3; *L'Art musical* (March 11, 1938), [591]; *Der Bund* (March 17, 1938), 3; René Dumesnil, "Julie Reisserova," *Mercure de France*, vol. CCLXXXIV,

Vítězslava Kaprálová mentioned it in an undated letter to her parents where she said that she felt very sorry and "spent the whole evening reminiscing with Martinů."[85] (When and where Reisserová and Kaprálová first met is unknown.)

Several events paid tribute to the deceased, notably in Denmark, France, and Czechoslovakia. On April 11, 1938, the Danish radio broadcast a commemorative concert in which Inger Raasløff sang *Pod sněhem* and *Světlo* accompanied by Folmer Jensen on the piano, and Erik Tuxen conducted the *Suita* and the *Pastorale maritimo*.[86] Two other concerts were programmed in Paris. The first – given in honor of the Czech composer "of great talent ... who, in many circumstances, gave precious proof of her attachment to France and our musicians" – took place at the Revue musicale (70, avenue Kléber) on April 26, 1938. Accompanied on the piano by Maroussia Orloff, Gilberte Arvez-Vernet sang the song cycles *Pod sněhem* and *Březen*.[87] The second was organized by the "Friends of Julie Reisserová" ("Amis de Julie Reisserova"), in the concert hall of the École Normale de Musique two days later on Thursday April 28, in the presence of several Czech representatives, including the plenipotentiary Štefan Osuský and his wife. Victor Tapié, a professor of history at the University of Lille, opened the concert with an address in which he recounted the too short career of the musician. Stan Golestan, then professor of composition at the École Normale, penned a moving account of the evening:

> Julie Reisserova, femme de cœur, ardente artiste, disparue récemment, arrachée à ses amis et à son art de la composition, a su, par son goût de la culture, se hausser au rang des maîtres sérieux. Ses œuvres dessinent des aspects multiples: musique d'orchestre, musique de chambre; œuvres pour piano, jouées cette fois par Mme A. van Barentzen. *Esquisses*, évoquant des traits impressionnistes. *Sous la neige* et *Giboulées de mars*, cycles de mélodies descriptives, depuis la touchante mélancolie jusqu'au charme des joies slovaques, que Mme Arveg-Vernet [sic] a mis en relief avec une saisissante expression. Au programme, un autre hommage significatif fut rendu aux maîtres qui présidèrent à l'éducation de Mme Julie Reisserova; Josepk [sic] Suk et Albert Roussel, avec les deux Trios respectifs, piano et cordes, exécutés soigneusement par A. van Barentzen, Dany Brunschwig et A. Heuclin [recte André Huvelin].[88]

49th year, no. 959 (June 1, 1938), 457; *Československo-jihoslovanská revue*, vol. 8, nos. 3–4 (1938), 94; *Muzički glasnik*, 4 (1938), 83; *L'Europe centrale*, 13th year (1938), 175.

[85] Karla Hartl (ed.), *Vítězslava Kaprálová: Dopisy domů: korespondence rodičům z let 1935–1940* (Toronto: The Kapralova Society, 2015), 146: "Bylo mně jí moc líto a celý večer jsme s Martinů provzpomínali." The letter may have been written on or around March 7, 1938. The two women were ranked among the best composers in the *Pravda* (October 23, 1948), 4.

[86] *Národní politika* (April 10, 1938), 8.

[87] "Les auditions du midi de la Revue musicale," *La Revue musicale*, vol. 19 no. 185 (July–August, 1938), 65: "... de grand talent et qui, en maintes circonstances, a donné des preuves précieuses de son attachement à la France et à nos musiciens."

[88] Stan Golestan, "Musique tchèque: La commémoration d'une artiste disparue," *Le Figaro* (May 9, 1938), 4. See also *Journal des débats politiques et littéraires* (April 28, 1938), 4;

Julie Reisserová, a woman of heart, an ardent artist, who recently passed away, torn from her friends and her art of composition, was able, through her taste for culture, to rise to the rank of serious masters. Her works trace multiple genres: orchestral music, chamber music; works for piano, played this time by Mrs. A. van Bärentzen. *Esquisses*, evoking impressionist features. *Sous la neige* [*Pod sněhem*] and *Giboulées de mars* [*Březen*], cycles of descriptive *mélodies*, from the touching melancholy to the charm of Slovakian joys, which Mrs. Arvez-Vernet highlighted with striking expression [accompanied by Mrs. Blanchard de Chatillon]. On the program, another significant tribute was paid to the masters who presided over the education of Mrs. Julie Reisserová; Josef Suk and Albert Roussel, with the two respective Trios, piano and strings carefully performed by A. van Bärentzen, Dany Brunschwig, and A. Heuclin [*recte* André Huvelin].

According to Élisabeth de Mondésir, Marie Tymichová, from the Paris Opera, danced that evening to *La Bise* – played on the piano – with a rich inventiveness of turns, and Mrs. O. Guerfort sang *Février* (*Předjaří*).[89] René Dumesnil, who attended this last concert, echoed the general opinion on the works of the departed: they "express a nobility of spirit and a remarkable distinction as well as a deep sincerity. And it is these qualities, indeed, that all those who knew her and who today deplore her end appreciated in her."[90]

In Prague, the Women's National Council in cooperation with the Society for Musical Education and the Institute of Scandinavian and Dutch Education held an evening on April 26, 1938 in the hall of the Women's Club (26 Ve Smečkách Street). Josefa Hrdinová presented the event; compositions by Reisserová were performed by Zdeňka Ziková (soprano), Hans Walter Süsskind (piano), and the Singing Association of Prague Female Teachers, while some of her poems were recited by Karel P. Jelínek and Marguerite Houllé Renoir.[91] Other concerts of Reisserová's music took place in Prague during the following months and years. The Society for Contemporary Music, "The Present" ("Přítomnost"), opened its 1938–1939 season with a concert given in October where *Pod sněhem* was sung and praised for its lyricism.[92] On February 23, 1940, a tribute concert marking the second anniversary of the composer's death was held in the Umělecká Beseda Hall. The event was introduced by Jiřina Vacková, who presented the

---

Národní listy (May 6, 1938), 5; *Národní politika* (April 10, 1938), 8; Dumesnil, "Julie Reisserova," 457.

[89] Élisabeth de Mondésir, "Hommage à J. Reisserova," *L'Art musical* (May 6, 1938), 781. See also M. S., "Pařížska pocta Julii Reisserové," *Národní listy* (May 6, 1938), 5.

[90] Dumesnil, "Julie Reisserova," 457: "Ses œuvres ... expriment une noblesse d'esprit et une distinction remarquable en même temps qu'une sincérité profonde. Et ce sont ces qualités, en effet, qu'apprécièrent en elle tous ceux qui l'ont connue et qui déplorent aujourd'hui sa fin."

[91] *Národní listy* (April 22, 1938), 2; *Lidové noviny* (April 26, 1938), 10. Zdeněk Václav Tobolka, *Naučný slovník aktualit 1939: Ročník druhý* (Prague: L. Mazáč, 1939), 447.

[92] *Národní politika* (October 21, 1938), 6.

life and work of the musician with – according to the chronicler of the *Národní politika* – an overly biased view.[93] Marie Zupancová then sang the cycles *Pod sněhem* and *Březen*, accompanied by Otakar Vondrovic, who also played the *Esquisses*.[94] The last tribute concerts recorded were given in Prague on February 25 and May 12, 1941, at the instigation of "The Circle of Friends of Julie Reisserová" and the Czech Women's Club.[95]

The soprano Marie Zupancová [Zupanecová] – née Bodláková – had already sung *Březen* in the symphonic and piano accompaniment versions at least three times (on November 16, 1927, November 21, 1930, and February 7, 1932), and was thus in close contact with the Reissers. Jan married Zupancová on April 29, 1939 (Figure 3), but almost nothing is known about her. The Czech press recorded some of her public appearances between the late 1920s and early 1940s.[96] Daughter of Rudolf Bodlák and born on April 26, 1906,[97] she had an honorable career as an opera singer, notably at the Velká opereta (Great Operetta Theater) in Prague, and at the Operas of České Budějovice and Plzeň.[98] Ranked among the artists with exceptional qualities by Brazilian critics,[99] she resumed her singing activity in 1949 when she was released from diplomatic protocol.[100] In her recitals, she liked to program – among other pieces by Smetana, Dvořák, Mahler, Richard Strauss, Wolf, and Mussorgsky – *mélodies* by Roussel, Martinů, and Reisserová's *Jaro v ulici*.[101] In Rio de Janeiro, the couple lived in a sumptuous apartment on Avenue Atlântica,[102] where they had parties during which Marie sang old Czech songs and Jan told of the old days and customs of his country. The former diplomat remained active as President of the Brazilian Red Cross Refugee Aid Organization and Executive Vice-President of the Brazilian Center for a Free Europe. In 1968,

---

[93] More on this in section 5, and note 250.
[94] *Národní politika* (February 23, 1940), 6; *Národní politika* (February 25, 1940), 8.
[95] *Lidové noviny* (February 27, 1941), 7; *Lidové noviny* (May 12, 1941), 2.
[96] *Národní listy* (November 29, 1929), 4; *Národní politika* (December 29, 1929), 9; *Národní listy* (March 31, 1930), 2; *Národní politika* (April 23, 1931), 4; *Lidové noviny* (March 20, 1941), 7; *Národní listy* (April 29, 1941), 5.
[97] *Diário Oficial da União* (June 1966), section 1, 14. Jan and Marie Reisser became naturalized Brazilians in June 1966.
[98] *Linie*, 2nd year, no. 6 (January 1933), 43; *Jihočeské listy* (June 3, 1933), 3; *Jihočech* (January 5, 1933), 5.
[99] Dyla Josetti, "Maria Reisserová," *A Manhã* (November 20, 1949), 3; *O Jornal* (June 28, 1956), 8.
[100] Antonio Bento, "O festival de Maria Reisserová," *Diario Carioca* (November 18, 1949), 6; Eurico Nogueira França, "Musica: Recital da cantora Reisserová," *Correio da Manhã* (November 18, 1949), 15.
[101] *Jornal do Commercio* (November 16, 1949), 6; *A Manhã* (March 29, 1950), 3; *O Jornal* (June 28, 1956), 8.
[102] Avenida Atlântica no. 762 ("Califórnia" building), Apartment no. 302, Rio de Janeiro; see *Jornal do Commercio* (June 12, 1979), 6. In 1979, Jan and Marie Reisser's apartment was evaluated at 800,000.00 reals. They also owned a membership certificate from the Touring Club of Brazil worth 2,000.00 reals, and ten shares of the Center Hotel evaluated at 15,000.00 reals.

Julie Reisserová (1888–1938) 21

Figure 3 From left to right: Marie Pauková (secretary of the Czech legation), Marie Bodláková (mother-in-law of Jan Reisser), Marie Bodláková-Reisserová (Jan Reisser's second wife) and Jan Reisser at their arrival in Rio de Janeiro, with Minister Carlos Martins Thompson Flores, and Jiri Reiszman (1946). Image courtesy of the National Library of Brazil; call-number: FM-1–9–020. A copy is available at the Archives of the Czech Ministry of Foreign Affairs, Personal files 1945–92, Box 816, "Reisser, Jan, JURDr." Originally published in *Tribuna Popular* (May 26, 1946), 8.

Reisser was still fighting from Brazil for freedom in his home country.[103] They finally moved – permanently? – to the north, to Teresópolis. Marie Bodláková-Reisserová died around November 11, 1973,[104] and Jan Reisser on January 24, 1975, in Rio de Janeiro.[105]

From this biographical study, it can be concluded that Julie Reisserová was a gifted musician who, thanks to her marriage to a member of the Czech diplomatic staff, had the good fortune to live in various European capitals and have her music programmed there. This brought her international recognition that even crossed the Atlantic Ocean, a recognition that was not granted to many women composers of her time. As a matter of fact, she was the first Czech woman musician whose works were known outside her native country. Until 1938, her name and works were mentioned or discussed in around 200 different

---

[103] *O Jornal* (September 29, 1968), 7.   [104] *Jornal do Brasil* (November 11, 1973), 42.
[105] Vana Verba, "Jan Reisser," *O Cruzeiro: Revista* (February 12, 1975), 31; *O Globo* (January 29, 1975), 10. On the occasion of his seventieth birthday, a short biography of Reisser was published in *O Jornal* (September 10, 1961), 7.

newspapers and magazines printed in Austria, Belgium, Czechoslovakia, Denmark, England, Finland, France, Germany, Hungary, Norway, Poland, Sweden, Switzerland, the United States, and Yugoslavia. Yet, her musical compositions are not numerous, not only because of her self-censorship and social duties, but also because like her mentor and friend Roussel, she began the study of composition rather late in life (around the age of thirty), thus confirming Nadia Boulanger's belief that great artists are not always child prodigies.[106]

3 Reisserová and Feminism

During her teenage years, Julie Reisserová was said to be a true beauty wooed by young men. Her eyes were brown and expressive, her hair a golden brown.[107] According to Jan Reisser's unpublished memoirs *Léta s Julkou* (*Years with Julie*) – as a distinguished World War II resistance veteran – he possibly attempted to integrate his late wife into the collective memory of national heroes:[108]

> ... žádnému fotografovi se nepodařilo zachytit skutečný výraz její tváře, poněvadž jeho tajemství spočívalo v pohybu. Také celá Julčina osobnost byla v neustálém pohybu – proto se jí vždy tolik líbilo heslo starořecké filosofie Herakleitovy "Všecko plyne."
>
> Julka byla stvořena ze samých protikladů a nikdo nemohl si býti jist, jaká bude její reakce na nejbližší událost nebo myšlenku ...
>
> Z komplexu protikladů (too many schools – tomu říkávala Julka) dvě složky zcela protichůdné vystupovaly v její povaze nejzřejměji. Existovala Julka brilantní a Julka timidní.
>
> Navenek dominuje brilantnost. Julka jako mladá dívka vstupuje do společnosti t. zv. Pražské zlaté mládeže se všemi nároky býti jednou z nich, nákladně se obléká, hraje tenis na Štvanici ... Chce oslňovat, je ráda středem společnosti, k čemuž jí dopomáhá její bystrá reakce, parátnost v konversaci a břitký vtip. Tato Julka je tvorem luxusním a mondenním ...
>
> Ale ve symbiose s tímto tvorem žije Julka timidní! Julka, která se ostýchá vejíti do krámu, kde si má něco koupit, která se ostýchá býti představena někomu významnějšímu a při představování podávajíc ruku vždy učiní krok zpět místo kroku vpřed – charakteristický postoj, který ji provází po celý život. Tato Julka uzavírá se náhle na celá období vnějšímu světu, pouští se do studia jazyků, do dějin filosofie, dějin umění, hltá literaturu, píše básně, hraje klavír, tajně improvisuje.

---

[106] Bruno Monsaingeon, *Mademoiselle: Conversations with Nadia Boulanger*, translated by Robyn Marsack (Manchester: Carcanet Press Ltd, 1985), 41–43; Nadia Boulanger, "L'Œuvre théâtrale d'Albert Roussel," *Albert Roussel: Numéro spécial de la Revue musicale* (April 1929), 104.

[107] Hrdinová, "Julie Reisserová," [1].

[108] "Julkou" being the diminutive of Julie, the title could also be translated as "Years with my Julie."

> Tyto dvě hlavní linie v jejím charakteru vedou spolu ustavičný boj. Tím vzniká velká komplikovanost její osobnosti ...[109]
>
> Julka's whole personality was in constant motion – that is why she was always fond of the motto of the ancient Greek philosophy of Heraclitus, "Everything flows" [*panta rhei*].
>
> Julka was made of contradictions, and no one could be sure what her reaction to the next event or thought would be ...
>
> Out of the complex of contradictions (too many schools – Julka used to call it), two completely contradictory components stood out most clearly in her nature. These were Julka the brilliant and Julka the timid.
>
> Outwardly, brilliance dominates. As a young girl, Julka enters the society of the so-called golden youth of Prague with all the requirements of being one of them, dresses up, plays tennis at the Štvanice [an island on the river Vltava in Prague] ... She wants to dazzle, she likes to be the center of the society, which is helped by her quick-witted reactions, her conversation skills and sharp wit. This Julka is a luxurious and mundane creature ...
>
> But in symbiosis with this creature, Julka the timid lives! This Julka who is too shy to go into a shop to buy something, who is too shy to be introduced to someone more important, always takes a step backward instead of forward when shaking hands – a characteristic attitude that has been with her all her life. This Julka suddenly shuts herself off from the outside world for entire periods, embarks on the study of languages, the history of philosophy, the history of art, devours literature, writes poems, plays the piano, improvises in secret.
>
> These two main lines in her character are in constant struggle with each other. This creates a great complexity in her personality.

This portrait – not devoid of clichés – shows an elegant, worldly, and perhaps a little superficial Julie, a talkative and witty young woman in her twenties who could spend hours alone reading, writing, and improvising at the piano. Elsewhere in his memoirs, Reisser confides that his wife had a romantic vision of love, full of pure emotion.[110] Besides, she was athletic, loved being outdoors, and seems to have taken great care with her appearance, as the photographs published in newspapers testify (Figure 4).[111] To believe written sources, Reisserová was refined, graceful, gentle, delicate and modest, but also a "charming hostess"[112] who enjoyed receiving visitors at the embassies she had tastefully furnished. On that matter, Reisser's hierarchy acknowledged that his professional and social behavior was irreproachable, and that his wife was

---

[109] Vacková, *Julie Reisserová*, 5–6.   [110] Vacková, *Julie Reisserová*, 13.
[111] On the photograph (1931) published in Závada, "Skladatelka Julie Reisserová o sobě," 44 (reproduced on the cover of my edition of Reisserová's music), she wears a fashionable fur coat, a hat and displays a broad smile. She is also very elegantly dressed in the photograph printed in *Berlingske tidende* (February 27, 1938), 5.
[112] *Dansk musiktidsskrift*, 13 (1938), 68: "charmerende værtinde."

24 Women in Music

† pí Julie Reisserová, nadaná
česká skladatelka, žačka Rous-
selova, jejíž orchestrální i pís-
ňové skladby byly s úspěchem
hrány u nás
i v cizině.

Figure 4 "Mrs. Julie Reisserová, a gifted Czech composer, a pupil of Roussel, whose [Reisserová's] orchestral and vocal compositions were successfully performed here and abroad."
Image courtesy of the National Library of the Czech Republic; call-number: 54 A 2313. Originally published in *Forum* (February 29, 1936), 19; *L'Art musical* (January 22, 1937), [378]; *Le Guide du Concert* (February 12, 1937), 515; *Neues Wiener Journal* (April 20, 1937), 7; *Pestrý týden* (March 12, 1938), 2.

"suitable for social relations and deportment."[113] She also played the piano very well and sang. In other words, she was a paragon of femininity in accordance with the stereotypes of her time.

If some journalists condescendingly associated Reisserová's name with her husband's profession, it must not be concluded that he made her career and that she remained in his shadow. On the contrary, she was solely responsible for her own success as a composer. As Gisela Urban insightfully wrote in the *Neues Wiener Journal*, "As splendidly as Julie Reisserová knows how to fulfill the social duties imposed on her as the wife of the Czechoslovak diplomat Dr. Jan Reisser, she must be appreciated first and foremost as a composer."[114] Whenever she was in the limelight, Jan Reisser stayed hidden. As opposed to the composer Louise Héritte-Viardot, Pauline Viardot-Garcia's eldest child who married a diplomat uninterested in music, Reisser always supported the career of his wife, gave her the freedom to devote herself to the arts, had faith in her achievements, and provided her with a particularly comfortable domestic life.[115] (He acted the same way with his second spouse, Marie Bodláková-Reisserová.) It is possible, however, that being the wife of a *chargé d'affaires* and a diplomat prevented male journalists from using overtly sarcastic rhetoric against her. Still, due to her social obligations and lack of time, she focused only on rather small-scale scores, although she stated in 1931 that she was very interested in orchestral music.[116]

3.1 Reisserová as Feminist

After the death of her father on July 4, 1905,[117] Reisserová decided to study foreign languages seriously, and passed the state exam to teach French and English. This may have prompted her to be a feminist activist. Indeed, before the founding of the Czechoslovak Republic in October 1918, a celibacy law – which remained officially in force until 1919 – forbade women instructors to marry and have children. This law not only impacted directly her future career as a teacher, but also that of her childhood friend, Josefa Hrdinová, who pursued the same objective.

To date, it is not known how Reisserová – and for that matter Hrdinová[118] – came into contact with the feminist milieu, but it can be surmised that Jan Reisser acted as

---

[113] "jeho choť vhodná pro společen styky a vystupování."
[114] Gisela Urban, "Komponistin und Diplomatenfrau," 7: "So prächtig Julie Reißerova die gesellschaftlichen Pflichten zu erfüllen versteht, die ihr als Gattin des tschechoslowakischen Diplomaten Dr. Jan Reißer auferlegt sind, in erster Reihe muß sie doch als Komponistin gewürdigt werden."
[115] Hrdinová, "Julie Reisserová," [2].   [116] "Dotazník," [2].
[117] Death register, Kostel sv. Štěpána (Church of Saint-Stephen), Prague City Archives, ŠT Z13, 216 (fol. 218v–219r); *Národní listy* (July 8, 1905), 8.
[118] Hrdinová worked in the field of women's education and Czech-French cultural relations. She edited the magazine *Škola a rodina* (*School and family*).

an intermediary. Both Reisser and Jan Masaryk entered the ministry of foreign affairs in 1919 where they became close friends.[119] The latter was the son of Tomáš Garrigue Masaryk, the first president of the new Republic. Under the impulse of President Masaryk, deep changes occurred in the constitution and the regulation of women's rights. Masaryk had a sophisticated understanding of Western culture, and of liberal French culture in particular. His wife, Charlotte Garrigue Masaryk, an American with Huguenot ancestry, had a strong influence on him.[120] Starting 1905, she became very active in the enfranchisement of women, became a member of various associations, such as the Central Association of Czech Women (Ústřední spolek českých žen), and worked hand in hand with one of the most prominent figures of the Czech feminist movement, the future senator Františka Plamínková.[121] She even played a key role in the writing of Article 106 of the Czechoslovak Constitution of 1920 enshrining equality between men and women.[122] The connection between Reisser and Masaryk may even have helped introduce Reisserová to Plamínková, the founder of the Women's National Council (Ženská národní rada) in 1923. This Council proved to be "the most influential lobbying group of women in Czechoslovakia ... and also became the voice of Czechoslovakia in a number of prominent international feminist organizations, including the International Council of Women."[123] It turned out that all these people were not only heavily involved in women's rights advocacy, but also very good amateur musicians and connoisseurs. Thus, the Ženská národní rada and its network were at the origin of at least seven concerts at which works by Reisserová were performed: in Belgrade on May 14, 1931; in Prague on October 23, 1931 (under the patronage of President Masaryk[124]), April 29, 1934, November 30, 1936, and December 3, 1937; in Vienna on April 23, 1937; and in Bratislava on March 3, 1937 (the latter event was organized by the association of college-educated women during which *Březen* was sung by Milada Jirásková).

Another hypothesis, which does not exclude the previous one, is that Jan Reisser introduced his wife to the feminist milieu through Bohumila Rosenkrancová with

---

[119] Jan Reisser published his short brochure *Jan Masaryk* (Rio de Janeiro: n.n., 1949) just after his friend's mysterious death.
[120] He even agreed to add his wife's last name to his own, which was very unusual in Czechoslovakia at the time.
[121] Barbara Reinfeld, "Františka Plamínková (1875–1942), Czech Feminist and Patriot," *Nationalities Papers*, 25 (March 1997), 13–33.
[122] Francisca de Haan, Krassimira Daskalova, and Anna Loutfi (eds.), *A Biographical Dictionary of Women's Movements and Feminisms: Central, Easter, and South Eastern Europe, 19th and 20th Centuries* (Budapest, New York: Central European University Press, 2006), 308.
[123] For this paragraph, see Melissa Feinberg, *Elusive Equality: Gender, Citizenship, and the Limits of Democracy in Czechoslovakia, 1918–1950* (Pittsburgh: University of Pittsburgh Press, 2006), 5–6, 11–40, 53.
[124] *Národní politika* (October 11, 1931), 9.

whom he studied singing. Plamínková and Rosenkrancová, who also taught Zdeňka Ziková and Marie Bodláková, knew each other. On the occasion of the twentieth anniversary of Rosenkrancová's artistic activities, the Prague publishing house Sfinx issued a collection of articles and drawings to which Plamínková, Reisserová, Ziková, Hana Benešová, and Vincent d'Indy among others, contributed.[125] Moreover, an audition of Rosenkrancová's students took place on November 16, 1927, during which Bodláková sang two songs from *Březen*.

It is probably through this feminist network that Reisserová got to know Anna (Aťa) Klecandová-Martenová – née Kopalová – with whom she had much in common. The latter graduated from the Minerva school, the first gymnasium for young Czech women in the Austro-Hungarian Empire, founded in Prague by Eliška Krásnohorská – the librettist of four of Smetana's operas – where female pupils were prepared to enter the university as full-time students. She continued her studies at Charles University focusing on ancient Indian philology, comparative linguistics, Arabic, and literature. She earned a doctorate in 1919, becoming the first female orientalist scholar. Kopalová first married the literary critic and writer Miloš Marten who died during World War I. Her second husband was General Vojtěch Vladimír Klecanda whose death in 1947 remains as mysterious as that of Jan Masaryk in 1948.[126] She traveled extensively with her husbands, especially to France and Italy, where General Klecanda served as military attaché at the Czech Embassy in Rome and Paris. Persuaded, as Reisserová seems to have been, that the success of an embassy depends on the ability of diplomats' wives to work together to promote their homeland, she held diplomatic salons, where she gave lectures on Czechoslovak culture, and more particularly on the Czech women's movement.[127] Thus, she organized a concert in Paris in November 1930, where music by Reisserová was performed.[128] It can also be surmised that Klecandová-Martenová introduced Reisserová to Paul Claudel's play *Partage de midi*, if not to Paul Claudel himself. Miloš Marten was acquainted with Claudel in Paris in 1907–1908, met him regularly when he was French consul in Prague between 1909 and 1911, and even asked him to be his best man at his wedding to Anna. In an interview, Reisserová confessed that one of her first attempts as a composer

---

[125] Jaroslav Maria (ed.), *Bohumila Rosenkrancová: památník vydaný k dvacetiletému jubileu umělecké činnosti Bohumily Rosenkrancové* (Prague: Sfinx, 1930). Plamínková also authored an article about the artist: Františka Plamínková, "Paní Bohumila Rosenkrancová," *Ženská rada*, 5th year, no. 1 (1929), 6.
[126] Both of them died by defenestration.
[127] Albína Honzáková (ed.), *Československé studentky let 1890–1930: Almanach na oslavu čtyřicátého výročí založení ženského studia Eliškou Krásnohorskou* (Prague: Ženská národní rada a Spolek Minerva, 1930), 271–276.
[128] *Národní listy* (November 26, 1930), 5.

(around 1919) was a setting of part of Claudel's *Partage de midi* (actually an orchestral overture to the play), and that this trial opened the doors to Josef Bohuslav Foerster.[129] If this anecdote is correct, Anna Klecandová-Martenová would have indirectly played a key role in Reisserová's musical career.

It was again thanks to the feminist milieu that Reisserová's music crossed the Atlantic Ocean. To celebrate Františka Plamínková's sixtieth birthday in 1936, she composed *Slavnostní den*, a work for women's chorus that was publicly premiered in Prague on December 3, 1937, by the Singing Association of Prague Female Teachers (Pěvecké sdružení pražských učitelek) under the direction of Metod Vymetal.[130] This vocal ensemble, founded in 1912 when women's singing was denigrated, had just won the Grand Prix at the 1937 World Exhibition in Paris. Following the concert, the score was accepted by Sophie Drinker to be given again in Philadelphia. It seems that the intermediary between Reisserová and Drinker was one of the choristers who sang *Slavnostní den*. Drinker was among the first people in the United States to research and promote the role of women in the history of music. In her seminal book published in 1948, *Music and Women: The Story of Women in Their Relation to Music*,[131] she sought to understand why women were condemned to be mere performers of men's music instead of using the language of music themselves to express their own ideas and feelings. (Reisserová also tackled this particular point in her 1937 lecture.) Like the Association of Prague mentioned previously, Drinker also encouraged choral singing by women by sponsoring the Montgomery Singers, a women's choir often directed by Lela Vauclain, which met every Wednesday morning in the large music room of her house.[132] *Slavnostní den* received its American premiere there in 1938. Interestingly enough, Julie Reisserová and Sophie Drinker were both married to jurists and amateur musicologists; Henry Sandwith Drinker is still known for translating German texts of vocal compositions by Schubert and Bach into English.[133]

3.2 Reisserová's Thoughts on Being a Woman Composer

On April 23, 1937, the Federation of Austrian Women's Associations (Bund Österreichischer Frauenvereine) – a member of the International Council of Women – arranged a lecture and concert evening on the theme "Women

---

[129] Závada, "Skladatelka Julie Reisserová o sobě," 44; "Dotazník," [1]: Reisserová dates the score to 1931; is this the year of a later revision?

[130] *Národní politika* (February 1, 1938), 7.

[131] Sophie Drinker, *Music and Women: The Story of Women in Their Relation to Music* (New York: Coward-McCann Inc., 1948).

[132] Ruth A. Solie, "Culture, Feminism, and the Sacred: Sophie Drinker's Musical Activism," in Ralph P. Locke and Cyrilla Barr (eds.), *Cultivating Music in America: Women Patrons and Activists Since 1860* (Berkeley, California: University of California Press, 1997), 290.

[133] Solie, "Culture, Feminism, and the Sacred," 270.

Musicians of the Present" ("Musikschaffende Frauen der Gegenwart") in the House of Industry in Vienna to promote women as composers. In front of a large audience Julie Reisserová, the keynote speaker of the event, delivered a much-appreciated lecture on the subject "The Woman as Composer" ("Die Frau als Komponistin;" Appendix A). The event – widely announced[134] – received significant coverage, and reports were published in *Die Österreicherin, Der Wiener Tag, Die Stunde*, and even in *Musical America*.[135]

Reisserová began her talk with the common romantic statement that "Music is the most immaterial of all arts, its world moves in dreamland. . . . Music is therefore the art that requires the greatest sensitivity from the author." Considering that the average woman possesses greater sensitivity than the average man (a personal point of view shaped by contemporany gender norms), she then posited that sensitivity is a major asset for women in the creation of music, and thus that women should be better composers than men. Tactfully (or shyly?), Reisserová did not insist upon this assertion, probably because it went against the opinion still widespread at the time – conspicuously publicized by Eduard Hanslik in *On the Musically Beautiful* and George Upton in his successful book *Woman in Music*[136] – that sensitivity is a weakness for women that prevents them from the concentration necessary for musical composition.[137] Nonetheless, she admitted – perhaps a little too quickly – that there were few well-known women composers by the 1930s (she failed to name them). In her opinion, shared by others, this was not due to a lack of abilities, but rather to historical development and social conditions.

Thanks to the women's movement that had grown in strength during the nineteenth and early twentieth centuries, women managed to assert themselves in a wide variety of professions. Yet, Reisserová acknowledged that if important women writers and painters are not uncommon, there are few women composers. She related this observation to the fact that education in literature, drawing, and painting has always been part of good society, and that it was enough to stimulate creative work to women with talent. On the contrary, if music lessons have also been part of a good education, they remained limited to learning how to play either violin or piano, or how to sing. That is why there are eminent female virtuosos and singers. But, as Reisserová put it, "In literature

---
[134] Notably in Czech-language Viennese newspapers such as *Pravda* (April 22, 1937), 1.
[135] *Die Österreicherin*, 10th year, no. 4 (May 1937), 1–2; Joseph Gregor, "Debüt einer belgischen Pianistin in Wien," *Neues Wiener Journal* (April 23, 1937), 10; A. R., "Musikschaffende Frauen der Gegenwart," *Der Wiener Tag* (April 25, 1937), 11; P. Stf., "Julie Reisserova über die Frau als Komponistin," *Die Stunde* (April 27, 1937), 4; Stefan, "Viennese Festival Weeks," 22.
[136] Eduard Hanslick, *On the Musically Beautiful*, translation from the eighth German edition by Geoffrey Paysant (Indianapolis: Hackett, 1986), 46; George Putnam Upton, *Woman in Music* (Chicago: A. C. McClurg and Company, 1892), 18–32.
[137] Lucy Green, *Music, Gender, Education* (Cambridge: Cambridge University Press, 1997), 14; Florence Launay, *Les compositrices en France au xixe siècle* (Paris: Fayard, 2006), 144.

and painting, women had always learned the basics for the productive, but in music only for the reproductive." This statement is in keeping with some gendered characteristics anchored in the popular belief that "femininity is defined as passive and reproductive."[138] For instance, George Eggleston already considered in 1883 that "the study of music, and especially the acquirement of practical skill in making music, is ... well recognized as a necessary part of a girl's education," and "as a means of adding to the attractiveness of her home."[139] Upton went even farther by claiming that a woman "will always be the recipient and interpreter, but there is little hope she will be the creator."[140]

In the second, more factual, pragmatic and autobiographical part of her lecture, Reisserová discussed her own career path, her years of study, and the "tremendous difficulties which a woman in particular has to overcome in order to prevail in the competition of today."[141] Fortunately, as Foerster recalls in his memoirs (in accordance with the gender stereotypes of his time), Reisserová combined the heightened sensitivity of a woman with a strong will and masculine strength.[142] The basic musical instruction mentioned in this section was obviously not enough for women to compose, because composing is inconceivable without a thorough study of theory. Music theory is a strict science, akin to mathematics and physics; and it was not until women began to learn other exact sciences that they started to devote themselves to composition. Women had indeed to wait until 1850 to be allowed to study theory and even composition at the Paris Conservatory, and 1877 at the Leipzig Conservatory.[143] Reisserová then acknowledged that in the late 1930s many women studied composition, and assumed that in the near future their number would steadily increase.[144] Nonetheless, she advised them to pen music without the ambition to compete with men, as Camille Saint-Saëns had already cautioned, quite disparagingly:

> Les femmes sont curieuses quand elles se mêlent sérieusement d'art: elles semblent préoccupées avant tout de faire oublier qu'elles sont femmes et de montrer une virilité débordante, sans songer que c'est justement cette préoccupation qui décèle la femme.[145]

---

[138] Green, *Music, Gender, Education*, 14.
[139] George Cary Eggleston, "The Education of Women," *Harper's New Monthly Magazine* (July 1883), 294.
[140] Upton, *Woman in Music*, 31.   [141] Stefan, "Viennese Festival Weeks," 22.
[142] Vacková, *Julie Reisserová*, 9.
[143] Launay, *Les compositrices en France*, 36; Eugene Gates, "The Woman Composer Question: Philosophical and Historical Perspectives," in Eugene Gates and Karla Hartl (eds.), *The Women in Music Anthology* (Toronto: The Kapralova Society, 2021), 14.
[144] Already in 1901, René Lara was alarmed by the growing number of female composers; *Le Figaro* (October 5, 1901), 2.
[145] Camille Saint-Saëns, *Harmonie et mélodie*, 2nd ed. (Paris: Calmann Lévy, 1885), 228 (about Augusta Holmès).

> Women are curious when they are seriously involved in art: they seem preoccupied above all with making people forget that they are women and with showing an overflowing virility, without realizing that it is precisely this preoccupation that reveals the woman.

On the contrary, she urged them to create only out of inner necessity with sincerity and humility, because "art, in deep humility before all the wonders of creation, mercilessly condemns everything that is inauthentic."[146] This warning may have been the result of the critical reception of her own *Esquisses*, completed in the same year that Martinů published his *Esquisses de danses*. While it is possible that this timing was a coincidence, the similarity of the titles raises questions. Consequently, in his – biased? – review of the scores, Robert Bernard could not help comparing the two pupils of Roussel at her expense.[147]

Reisserová went on to say that inventive aptitude alone is not enough to be able to compose, and that the act of composing requires some professionalism and a long period of study.[148] What she really meant by "Métier" remains unclear, but this word may have concealed her own weakness: she was very gifted and (according to Jan Reisser's memoirs) had a hard time understanding and accepting that theoretical studies are necessary,[149] as if such studies were "difficult" (i.e., boring?) for a gifted person. This is perhaps what Bernard alluded to in reviewing Reisserová's three *Esquisses*, when he blamed her for the lack of elegance of their musical craftsmanship ("facture"), but his assessment is weakened by the fact that he also reproched Martinů for his excessive use of rhetorical (i.e., mechanical?) developments. No matter what, musical ideas must indeed be arranged so as to make them comprehensible to others. Perhaps Reisserová, who loved to improvise, learned the hard way that "The greatest difficulty in creating music consists in writing it down" so that "the real sound corresponds to the inner sound conception of the creator." To achieve this, many years of study are needed to master harmony, counterpoint, formal theory, and instrumentation. (On this last point, it should be noted that Reisserová never used the trombone in her scores, because she thought it was not suitable for a woman.[150])

During her studies with Roussel, she wondered if she would always have the necessary strength to reach her dream. She conceded that to be a composer and conductor demands a great deal of abnegation, above all for women. She probably recounted her debut as a conductor in Switzerland when she evoked a woman

---

[146] In her interview with E. K., "Z rozhovorů s Julii Reisserovou," *Národní politika: Odpolední vydání* (October 20, 1931), 4, Reisserová claimed that only genuine talent can endure time.

[147] Robert Bernard, "Musiques diverses pour piano," *La Revue musicale*, vol. 17, no. 169 (November 1936), 367–368. Reisserová may also have had Foerster's *Esquisses de danse*, op. 48, or Smetana's *Skizzen*, op. 4 and op. 5, in mind.

[148] She already expressed this idea in Ursus, "Julie Reisserova," 19.

[149] Vacková, *Julie Reisserová*, 12.   [150] Vacková, *Julie Reisserová*, 12.

standing "in front of an orchestra for the first time at the rehearsal of her own work." She felt how people looked at her "with a mixture of politeness, mistrust, and ridicule." For Reisserová only competence counts at the podium, regardless of gender. Of course "even women can only impress with their musicality," but to impose their authority, composers – and women composers in particular – need something else besides talent and mastery of technique, that is, a great deal of "vitality." By "vitality," Reisserová meant that being a composer "consumes the whole soul and the whole person," and that "the love of art ... keeps one high, but at the same time consumes one." In other words, "Only a great love of art can offer a substitute for the many things that a woman in particular has to sacrifice."[151] Implicitly, this suggests that to be a professional composer, a woman has to choose between her artistic aspiration and being a good mother and a good wife, a choice that was the fate of all aristocratic and middle-class women of the time. For example, when Cécile Chaminade was asked in 1908 whether she preferred to be a composer or a woman, she answered "a composer. Between being a mother and being an artist, I prefer being an artist."[152] Reisserová was confronted with the same dilemma, because even though she did not have children, she did have many social constraints as a diplomat's wife.

To conclude her talk, she confessed that:

> Like every author, I have been asked several times how the ideas actually come. And like every author I have to answer that in such moments one feels like a medium through which an unknown power speaks.... But whom art has marked as its spokesman, he will not escape his fate. However, I would not like to give you the impression that I see only difficulties in this profession. The artist's path is a way of the cross, but there are also moments of redemption, moments of creation, [and] of purest joy.

Such a testimony calls to mind Goethe's concept of *dämonisch* that refers to the godlike power to pass on divine things to men,[153] and a concept that inspired Nietzsche, and even Richard Wagner,[154] since the latter once told his wife, Cosima, that "a musician, while composing, actually falls into a mad somnambulistic state."[155] Reisserová's confidence implies that women composers can also

---

[151] P. Stf., "Julie Reisserova über die Frau als Komponistin," 4: "Nur eine große Liebe zur Kunst kann Ersatz bieten für das viele, was gerade eine Frau da opfern muß."

[152] Quoted from Launay, *Les compositrices en France*, 150: "Compositeur: Entre être une mère et être une artiste, je préfère être une artiste."

[153] Plato, *Symposium*, 202e.

[154] Georges Liébert, *Nietzsche and Music*, translated by David Pellauer and Graham Parkes (Chicago: University of Chicago Press, 2004), 16.

[155] Cosima Wagner, *Die Tagebücher: Band 1: 1869–1873* (Berlin: Hofenberg, 2015), 144: "so ein Musiker, während er komponiert, verfällt eigentlich einem wahnsinnigen somnambulen Zustand."

experience flashes of genius at a time when genius was denied to them.[156] For the latter, the notion of genius was quite an issue at the turn of the century. Thus, when Vincent d'Indy encouraged Marguerite-Marie de Fraguier to continue her studies in composition, she became "haunted by the idea that a woman cannot have, at least in music, the creative genius."[157] It is not known if Reisserová ever asked herself this question, but she undoubtedly experienced the throes of creation and saw in it a kind of divine inspiration.[158] Her reference to the sixth scene of Act I of Hans Pfitzner's opera *Palestrina*, in which angels dictate the *Missa Papæ Marcelli* to the old master is revealing. According to Jan Reisser, she had an utterly romantic conception of genius, in which natural inspiration alone prevailed over technique and hard work; she preferred to delay the completion of a score in case of lack of ideas rather than to finish it mechanically by using theoretical rules.[159] Finally, Reisserová maintained that whether the artist is a man or a woman, only the quality of the talent is decisive for the resulting work of art. In short, it is that kind of heartfelt account of her activity as a composer that may have incited the female chronicler of *L'Écho de Paris* to describe her as "the great Czech female composer" as early as 1936.[160]

Reisserová's lecture, whose subject was delivered in "a particularly interesting and thoroughly personal way,"[161] was followed by a concert during which the illustrious pianist Aline van Bärentzen played her *Esquisses*, and Maria Hussa sang three of her songs. The three *Esquisses* were notably acclaimed that day for the plasticity of their themes and for their energy. All these "impressive and inspired compositions" were said to convincingly exemplify Reisserová's talent and maturity: her technique was considered as "exceptional, her style of composition modern, but without any inclination to scorn form or sacrifice tonality."[162] Works by some of the most famous contemporary Austrian women creators were also performed that evening, particularly pieces by Johanna Müller-Hermann, Mathilde von Kralik, and Lio Hans.

A critical reading of Reisserová's lecture makes it clear that it is almost impossible to distinguish between a score penned by a male composer and one

---

[156] See for instance, Otto Weininger, *Sex and Character*, authorized translation from the sixth German edition (London: William Heinemann; New York: G. P. Putnam's Sons, 1907), 113: "From genius itself, the common quality of all different manifestations of genious, woman is debarred."

[157] Marguerite-Marie de Fraguier, *Vincent d'Indy: Souvenirs d'une élève accompagnée de lettres inédites du maître* (Paris: Jean Naert, 1934), 58: "J'étais hanté par l'idée qu'une femme ne peut avoir, en musique tout au moins, le génie créateur."

[158] Vacková, "Ô, božské umění, děkuji ti!," VII.   [159] Vacková, *Julie Reisserová*, 11.

[160] *L'Écho de Paris* (October 27, 1936), 4: "la géniale compositrice tchèque."

[161] P. Stf., "Julie Reisserova gestorben," 3: "besonders interessant und durchaus persönlich behandelte."

[162] Stefan, "Viennese Festival Weeks," 22.

written by a female composer. To substantiate this, it is perhaps interesting to report the opinion of Élisabeth de Mondésir after listening to Reisserová's *Březen* and *Pod sněhem* in 1938. For the French female critic, these "poetic" song cycles convey the "dramatic and varied feeling of a female soul" animated by a "romantic torment."[163] Unfortunately, she failed to provide any technical evidence to underpin her judgment. That her view was biased by a kind of woman's solidarity, however, remains debatable. Indeed, Paul Le Flem did not enjoy *Březen*, going as far as to affirm that *Nostalgie* and *Jaro v ulici* were two "musical uselessness[es]."[164] Yet, this hiatus was clearly a matter of taste, and may not have been due to gender discrimination, particularly in France where male critics did not select their adjectives based on the sex of the composer being reviewed.[165] In a report of the concert given in Prague on April 29, 1934, to celebrate the fiftieth anniversary of the founding of the Prague Vocational Schools for Women's Professions (Odborné školy pro ženská povolání v Praze), Jelena Holečková-Heidenreichová likewise highlighted the issue of male versus female composers, and wrote in *Lada*, a periodical "for the interests of Czech women and girls":

> Jestliže jsme po prvé (tuším před dvěma lety) naslouchali jejím skladbám s oprávněnou zvědavostí, jak asi umí moderní žena vzít do ruky pero skladatelské, chtěli bychom se dnes již nadobro zbavit této otázky po "ženském" umění a chtěli bychom ve skladbách Reisserové slyšeti jen hudbu projev, jeden z řady těch, kterým věnujeme pozornost jako soudobým, vývojově pokračujícím a sloužícím věčnému ideálu umění, bez ohledu na zajímavost a osudy osob.[166]

> If we first (two years ago, I think) listened to her [Reisserová's] compositions with a justified curiosity as to how a modern woman could possibly pick up a [male] composer's pen, we would now like to get rid of this question of "feminine" art for good, and would like to hear in Reisserová's compositions only the music of expression, one of the many to which we pay attention as contemporary, continuing in development and serving the eternal ideal of art, regardless of the interest and fate of the persons.

Julie Reisserová probably entered Prague feminist circles shortly before World War I, where she met the leading Czech women activists of the time. The success of her musical compositions and her continual comings and goings

---

[163] Mondésir, "Hommage à J. Reisserova," 781: "sentiment dramatique et varié d'une âme féminine"; "un tourment romantique."

[164] Paul Le Flem, "Un concert d'ouvrages inédits," *Comœdia* (April 28, 1929), 2: "inutilité musicale."

[165] Laura Hamer, *Female Composers, Conductors, Performers: Musiciennes of Interwar France, 1919–1939* (Abingdon, New York: Routledge, 2018), 40.

[166] Jelena Holečková-Heidenreichová, "Skladatelka Julie Reisserová," *Lada: list pro zájmy českých žen a dívek*, 56th year, no. 20 (1934), 318.

in Europe propelled her to the forefront of the international feminist scene, of which she became one of the standard-bearers. In this respect, the lecture she gave in Vienna proved to be an important milestone in her promotion of women as composers. If the ideas she developed are far from being all original – they were already the subject of heated debates in Europe and the United States at the end of the nineteenth and the beginning of the twentieth century[167] – they testify to her knowledge and involvement in them. The evocation of her personal experience, however, offers another perspective: it gives a touching and unique glimpse into her innermost artistic feelings, and provides some information on her working method, in which a demonic inspiration – often denied to women composers – has its part. Finally, her point that "music [i]s enhanced sensibility and that actually women, therefore, as the more sensitive would have to be even better composers than men"[168] did not go unnoticed and evidently struck the male correspondent of *Musical America*, as well as that of *Der Stunde* and of *Der Wiener Tag*.

4 Musical Works

Reisserová composed between 1923 and 1936. Her reputation rested on only seven works, the last – *Předjaří* – being the first of an unfinished song cycle for coloratura soprano and orchestra. During her formative years, she no doubt created several other pieces that no longer exist.[169] For example, in the early 1930s she declared that she had composed two male choirs, an orchestral overture to Claudel's play *Le Partage de midi*, and that she was working on a string quartet. Among the now lost papers she left behind after her death was a sketchbook containing other compositions, but Vacková did not supply details.[170] Since press clippings also provide imprecise titles of works, care should be taken when compiling Reisserová's catalog (Appendix B). Thus, it is likely that "Dvě melodie" and "Deux mélodies" ("Two Songs"), respectively found in the interview published in *Rozpravy Aventina* and in *La Semaine à Paris*, make reference to already known scores, as chroniclers may have used these phrases in the context of the 1927 concert at La Sorbonne to name *Za svítání*, *Světlo* and/or *Nostalgie*. Hence, only the song *Jarní* (*Spring*), the two piano pieces *Pramen* [*La Source*] (*The Source*)[171] and *Vítr* [*Le Vent*] (*The Wind*)

---

[167] Gates, "The Woman Composer Question," 3–29.
[168] Stefan, "Viennese Festival Weeks," 22.
[169] According to Hrdinová ("Julie Reisserová," 49), Reisserová was among the most prolific Czech composers; in "In memoriam Julija Reisserova," *Muzički glasnik*, 4 (1938), 83, Vaclav Vedral alludes to a large number of *mélodies* with piano accompaniment and choirs.
[170] Vacková, *Julie Reisserová*, 13.
[171] Work titles are given first in Czech; Reisserová's translations into French and/or German are then placed in square brackets.

played in Paris in 1927, as well as *Deux Allegros pro Klavír* can definitely be added to her list of works.[172] The following section deals with the reception of these works and their performance history.

4.1 Březen

Březen [*Giboulées de Mars*; *März*] (*March*) is the oldest preserved score by Julie Reisserová. This cycle was composed and orchestrated in Bern between 1923 and 1925. Three of its four songs were conceived while she was studying composition with Hohlfeld. The first to be written was *Světlo* [*Lumière*; *Das Licht*] (*Light*) on a poem originally penned in German by the composer herself and dedicated to her brother Vojtěch. This song was followed by *Za svítání* [*À l'Aube*; *In der Frühe*] (*Early Morning*) on verses by Eduard Mörike,[173] dedicated to the soprano Marie Žaludová-Knittlová, and *Nostalgie* (*Nostalgia*) on a text by the Japanese poet Ōshikōchi no Mitsune ("Ochi," 859–907) whose author of the translation remains unknown, dedicated to another celebrated opera artist, Zdeňka Ziková.[174] The last song composed was *Jaro v ulici* [*Printemps dans la rue*; *Frühling in der Strasse*] (*Spring in the Street*) on a French poem by Reisserová. She drafted it shortly after beginning her studies with Roussel. The song, dedicated to Anna Klecandová-Martenová, is influenced by French impressionism, and the ballets of Igor Stravinsky in particular. Later, the composer herself translated all the texts into German, French, and Czech to ensure a better distribution of *Březen* throughout Europe. The Danish version translated by Else West Neuhard was most likely commissioned by the Danish publisher Skandinavisk og borups Musikforlag at the time of the publication of the vocal score in 1934.[175] Three texts narrate the passage from the dark night of winter to the bright light of spring, and to the awakening of amorous desire, while *Jaro v ulici* describes the lover who frantically seeks his mate in the street.[176]

---

[172] These titles come from Závada, "Skladatelka Julie Reisserová o sobě," 44; *La Semaine à Paris* (March 4–11, 1927), 36; P. V., "Julie Reisserova," *Le Guide du Concert* (February 12, 1937), 515; Holečková-Heidenreichová, "Za Julií Reisserovou," 61–62 and 80; and from the advertisement reproduced at the end of the Danish print of the scores of *Březen* (1934) and *Esquisses* (1935). *Vítr* is also mentioned in *Národní politika* (February 25, 1927), [3]. It cannot be ruled out that the *Deux Allegros* were revised versions of *Pramen* and *Vítr*.

[173] This poem was often set to music, notably by Pauline Viardot (1865), and Hugo Wolf (1888).

[174] It is hardly possible to know in which language Reisserová first read this poem. The most common version then available in Europe was that of the poet Hans Bethge, "Die Wildgans," in *Japanischer Frühling: Nachdichtungen japanischer Lyrik* (Leipzig: Insel Verlag, 1918), 47. This collection was reprinted many times.

[175] The publication is announced in *Národní listy* (May 5, 1935), 11.

[176] All the poems set to music by the composer are reproduced in Jean-Paul C. Montagnier (ed.), *Julie Reisserová: Musique de chambre/Chamber Music* (Berlin: Ries & Erler, 2023), xiii–xix.

According to the surviving sources, *Za svítání*, *Nostalgie*, and *Světlo* were sung in public – in a version with piano accompaniment – as early as 1927, notably in Paris on February 24 and March 17 as part of concerts of Czech music, and then at the Mozarteum in Prague on November 16. Three other performances took place in 1928 in Paris, Geneva, and Bern. Worthy of note is the one held on April 28, 1928, during a dinner organized by the Cercle de la presse at the Club International de Genève, where Reisserová and Maria Jensen-Milliet sang *Za svítání* and *Světlo*, which were judged to be "original and engaging."[177] Jane Bathori, accompanied on the piano by Denyse Molié, gave the first documented public audition of *Jaro v ulici* on March 22, 1929, in Bern, along with *Světlo* and *Nostalgie*. The orchestral version of *Nostalgie* and *Jaro v ulici* was apparently given for the first time in Paris by Lydia de Rivera and the Orchestre du Conservatoire conducted by Marius-François Gaillard on April 23, 1929, but it did not appeal to the critic Paul Le Flem.[178] This version was then performed again in Bern by Violette Andreosi under the direction of Albert Neff on April 2, 1930. The first complete performance of the cycle in its symphonic version – patronized by the Women's National Council – took place in Prague on October 23, 1931, with Marie Žaludová-Knittlová and the Czech Philharmonic Orchestra conducted by Pavel Dědeček. According to the columnist of the *Národní listy* of October 31: "The song cycle with orchestra, entitled *Březen*, is composed to her [Reisserová's] own texts, but the composer definitely stands above the poetess in her choice of expression. With a beautifully sonorous, refined voice and a heartfelt delivery, Mrs. Žaludová gave her best to the four songs of the cycle."[179] Numerous other presentations of the cycle followed in both versions (with orchestra or with piano), especially in Copenhagen, which probably led the Danish publisher mentioned earlier in this section to distribute the vocal score.

In an interview, Reisserová confided that she had intended the cycle as a suite for orchestra with solo soprano (this statement is supported by the fact that *Nostalgie* begins with an orchestral prelude of twenty-two measures before the voice enters):

> Cyklus písní *Březen* tvoří čtyři čísla : *Za svítání*, *Světlo*, *Nostalgie* a *Jaro v ulici*. *Za svítání* je úvodní větou cyklu, plnou přízraků noci, impetuoso s uklidněním v andante esspressivo [sic]. *Světlo* je těžko-myslnou meditací

---

[177] *Journal de Genève* (April 29, 1928), 6: "originales et prenantes." The wording is so confusing that it is unclear who actually sang and who accompanied on the piano.

[178] Le Flem, "Un concert d'ouvrages inédits," 2.

[179] *Národní listy* (October 31, 1931), 4: "Cyklus písní s orkestrem, nadepsaný *Březen*, je komponován na vlastní texty, ale tu komponistka vybíravostí výrazu rozhodně stojí nad básnířkou. Krásně zvučným, kultivovaným hlasem i vroucně procítěným přednesem dopo[r]učila pi Žaludová čtyři písně cyklu co nejlépe."

> zimy, do níž náhle zableskne paprsek světla. *Nostalgie* tvoří přechod z těžkých nálad zimy prvních dvou písní k březnovému předjaří. *Jaro v ulici* znamená vítězství jara, světla a ruchu života a tvoří závěrečné "presto" v cyklu.
>
> Písně si představuji jako cyklus, poněvadž mají jednotnou, moji oblíbenou náladu předjaří. Cyklus je komponován spíše jako suita pro orchestr a sopránové solo.[180]
>
> The *Březen* song cycle consists of four numbers: *Za svítání, Světlo, Nostalgie,* and *Jaro v ulici. Za svítání* is the opening movement of the cycle, full of the phantoms of the night, impetuoso [mm. 1–33] with a calm in the andante espressivo [mm. 34–62]. *Světlo* is a heavy-minded meditation on winter, into which a ray of light suddenly flashes. *Nostalgie* forms the transition from the heavy winter moods in the first two songs to spring in March. *Jaro v ulici* signifies the victory of spring, light and the bustle of life, and forms the final "presto" in the cycle.
>
> I imagine the songs as a cycle because they have a uniform mood, my favorite mood of early spring. The cycle is composed more like a suite for orchestra and soprano solo.

Reisserová suggests here that the order of the songs was originally different from that transmitted by the published scores, an order that corresponded better to the poetic-musical description of the passage from winter to spring: *Za svítání, Světlo, Nostalgie,* and *Jaro v ulici.* The new sequence of the songs in the scores responds to another program aiming to relate the cycle to a symphony with soprano. The four songs are indeed like four movements of contrasting character: *Za svítání* is dramatic and *Nostalgie* lyrical, *Jaro v ulici* is like a scherzo, and *Světlo* provides a hymn-like conclusion.[181]

4.2 Suita

The *Suita* for orchestra, "dedicated to Albert Roussel in deepest gratitude" ("Dédié à Albert Roussel en profonde reconnaissance"), and originally titled *Letní den* (*Summer's Day*), was composed between 1924 and 1931 and was "published" in Copenhagen probably around 1934. The third movement, Allegro con moto, is the earliest in the order of composition and was written in Bern in 1924, then revised between 1927 and 1929. It was performed several times under the title *La Bise*. A first version was played on January 31, 1927, as part of an evening of Slavic dance organized by Lydia Wisiaková at the Lucerne Theater,[182] thus suggesting that the piece was initially conceived as

---

[180] Závada, "Skladatelka Julie Reisserová o sobě," 45. See also Hrdinová, "Julie Reisserová," 49.
[181] Vacková, *Julie Reisserová*, 17. The author cites in a note the program distributed during the concert given on September 12, 1936 in Prague by the Interallied Federation of Veterans.
[182] Vacková, *Julie Reisserová*, 53.

a choreographic work.[183] *La Bise* was then given several times at the Montreux Casino in 1928 and in 1929.[184] On the other hand, when it was produced for the first time in Paris, at the concert of Sunday April 23, 1929, at the Salle Gaveau under the direction of Marius-François Gaillard, Paul Le Flem considered that "*La Bise*, by M[rs.] Reisserová, is hardly distinguished by any salient qualities: banal ideas, harmonization and orchestra without flavor."[185] The piece was danced again to a piano version – played by Mrs. Blanchard de Chatillon – by Marie Tymichová on April 28, 1938, at the École Normale de Musique de Paris during the commemorative evening held by the French friends of Julie Reisserová.[186] The other two movements of the *Suita*, Allegro giocoso and Andantino espressivo, were begun around 1930 and completed during the summer of 1931 in Varengeville-sur-Mer.[187] It is not out of the question that the composer may also have taken advantage of this time to revise the score of *La Bise* one last time.

The *Suita* was performed in its entirety for the first time in public on October 23, 1931, at the Lucerna Palace in Prague by the Czech Philharmonic Orchestra under the direction of Pavel Dědeček, along with *Březen*, and Roussel's *Pour une fête de printemps*, op. 22. The press was particularly complimentary. After pointing out that several of the Czech artist's compositions had already been noted abroad and that Roussel had a decisive influence on Reisserová's art, the journalist of the *Národní listy* continued: "The three-movement orchestral suite *Letní den* [*Suita*] shows that the composer really has something to say, that she is capable of expressing herself distinctively and tastefully, and that she has also successfully mastered the technical side of composition."[188] In an interview for the same newspaper, Roussel stated that his student's compositions have "an undeniable charm and freshness, especially in the orchestral suite."[189] The *Suita* was given again successfully in Belgrade by the Belgrade Philharmonic Orchestra under the direction of Stefan Hristić on

---

[183] In 1931, Reisserová said that *La Bise* was a dance: Závada, "Skladatelka Julie Reisserová o sobě," 45. In *Národní politika* (February 25, 1927), [3], the work is confusingly referred to as *Vítr*. (Reisserová clearly differentiated *La Bise* from *Vítr* in her interview with Závada.)

[184] *Národní listy* (February 22, 1929), 5.

[185] Le Flem, "Un concert d'ouvrages inédits," 2: "*La Bise*, de Mme Reisserova ne se signale guère par des qualités saillantes: idées banales, harmonisation et orchestre sans saveur." See also *Guide du concert et des théâtres lyriques*, 15th year, no. 29 (April 19, 1929), 840.

[186] Mondésir, "Hommage à J. Reisserova," 781; M. S., "Pařížská pocta Julii Reisserové," *Národní listy* (May 6, 1938), 5.

[187] Závada, "Skladatelka Julie Reisserová o sobě," 45.

[188] *Národní listy* (October 31, 1931), 4: "Třívětá orkestrální suita *Letní den* vydává svědectví, že komponistka má opravdu co říci, že dovede vyjadřovati se výrazně a vkusně a že také technickou stránku komposice úspěšně ovládá."

[189] *Národní listy* (October 23, 1931), 1: "Má nesporný šarm a svěžest, zejména v orchestrální suitě."

April 23, 1933,[190] then in Olomouc on April 12, 1935, in Prague on July 26, and in Karlovy Vary on November 7, 1936.[191] The *Suita* was also broadcast on Radio-Prague on February 7, 1932, and on November 19, 1935, under the direction of Otakar Jeremiáš,[192] and on the Danish radio during the commemorative concert of April 1938. It is not unlikely that the *Suita* was performed on other occasions for which information is lacking. Thus, it is known that the score was programmed in the capital of Serbia by the Belgrade Philharmonic Orchestra under the direction Mihailo Vukdragović.[193]

The concert of October 23, 1931, was of great importance for Reisserová's career, as it was the one that established her reputation in Czechoslovakia.[194] A few days before the concert, she granted an interview to Vilém Závada, during which she invoked the *Suita* and presented it as a kind of symphonic poem or musical diary:

> *Letní den* je orchestrální suita, kterou jsem dokončila o letošních prázdninách, když mě Ženská rada vyzvala, abych zaslala nějaké skladby na její podzimní koncert. Dříve již existovala orchestrální skladba *La bise*, která nyní tvoří třetí větu suity. Je to ozvuk nálady lemanského jezera, kde bisa začne zdánlivě neškodně a na konec se rozpoutá do závratného tempa. Skladba má dva motivy, jeden líbezný a druhý bouřlivý, tak jako jasný klid lemanského klimatu je na chvíli rozrušen bouří na jezeře. První věta allegro je veselá a chtěla bych, aby vzbudila bezstarostnou náladu campingu. Nepředstavuji si to nijak deskriptivně, nýbrž výrazově. Proto volím pro větu přísnou formu. Ta druhá věta je výrazem prožitých reminiscencí a stesku po domově, kterému však nemám čas se dlouho oddávat.[195]

> *Summer's Day* is an orchestral suite I finished composing during the last summer vacation [in Varengeville-sur-Mer] when the Council of Women invited me to send some pieces for its fall concert. There was an earlier orchestral piece, *La bise*, which is now the third movement of the suite. It echoes the atmosphere of Lake Leman, where the north wind [i.e., "la bise" in French] begins in a seemingly innocuous way and at the end breaks into a frantic tempo. The piece has two motifs, one graceful [mm. 1–19] and the other stormy [mm. 20–31], just as the luminous calm of the Leman climate is for a moment disturbed by the storm on the lake. The first movement allegro is joyful, and I would like it to evoke the carefree atmosphere of camping. I do not imagine it in any descriptive way, but in terms of expression. That is why

---

[190] Rikard Švarc, "Muzika u zemlji, Beogradska filharmonija," *Zvuk* (May 7, 1933), 262–263; Roksanda Pejović, *Koncertni život u Beogradu* (Belgrade: FMU, 2004), 273; *Prager Presse* (April 30, 1933), 8.
[191] Vacková, *Julie Reisserová*, 55–56; Appendix C.
[192] *Reichenberger Zeitung* (November 16, 1935), 8.
[193] Heidenreich, "Za Julií Reisserovou," 94.   [194] *Narod* (October 23, 1931), 3.
[195] Závada, "Skladatelka Julie Reisserová o sobě," 45. For another interview, see E. K., "Z rozhovorů s Julií Reisserovou," 4.

I chose a strict form for the movement. The second movement is an expression of memories and homesickness, which I do not have time to indulge in at length.

4.3 Esquisses

The gestation of the three *Esquisses* (*Sketches*) extends over several years. The third is the oldest. It was written in 1928 and premiered under the title *Allégresse* (*Jubilation*) during the recital that Denyse Molié gave at the Montreux Casino on July 14 of the same year.[196] The piece was revived under this title on several occasions, notably by Molié and Emil Hájek in Bern, Belgrade, and Prague until 1932. That year, in Varengeville-sur-Mer, Reisserová added two other pages to it, *Esquisses* nos. 1 and 2, to constitute all that we know. This collection of piano pieces – i.e., the "Klavírní suit[a]" mentioned in Závada's interview?[197] – and its title are not insignificant, and obviously refer to the five *Esquisses de danses* that Martinů published in 1932. These works were naturally reviewed together in *La Revue musicale*. If the style of Reisserová was judged as "not as homogeneous and [her] invention as personal and ingenious" as those of her compatriot, her *Esquisses* were nevertheless viewed as "pleasant, welcome pages, and on the whole sympathetic and of an authentic musicality."[198] For Élisabeth de Mondésir, the musical ideas contained in the *Esquisses* were fresh and poetic,[199] whereas the chronicler of the *Národní politika* saw in them traditional ideas clothed in modern harmonies.[200] As for the reporter of *Der Wiener Tag*, the *Esquisses* were "characterized by an exemplary piano writing, flexible thematic and a lively pulsating motoric sensibility. Especially the powerful third piece must be called a valuable enrichment of the modern pianistic literature."[201] These pieces are thus in keeping with *Vítr*, whose harmonic boldness, rhythmic subtlety, and original melodic invention were hailed by the Swiss press.[202] The three *Esquisses* are respectively dedicated to the pianists who played them all over Europe: Aline van Bärentzen, Emil Hájek, and Denyse Molié.

---

[196] In June according to "Dotazník," [1].
[197] Závada, "Skladatelka Julie Reisserová o sobě," 45.
[198] Bernard, "Musiques diverses pour piano," 368: "La pensée est loin d'être aussi ramassée, le style aussi homogène et l'invention aussi personnelle et ingénieuse … Ce sont pourtant des pages agréables, bienvenues, et dans l'ensemble, sympathiques et d'une authentique musicalité."
[199] Mondésir, "Hommage à J. Reisserova," 781.   [200] *Národní politika* (February 27, 1937), 10.
[201] *Der Wiener Tag* (April 25, 1937), 11: "Sie zeichnen sich durch einen vorbildlichen Klaviersatz, plastische Thematik und lebendig pulsierendes motorisches Empfinden aus. Namentlich das kraftvolle dritte Stück muß als eine wertvolle Bereicherung der modernen pianistischen Literatur bezeichnet werden."
[202] Závada, "Skladatelka Julie Reisserová o sobě," 44.

4.4 Pastorale maritimo

The *Pastorale maritimo* was Reisserová's most critically acclaimed score, and her most popular orchestral work. If the title of the work may refer to Roussel's involvement in the French Navy and to the seascapes of the English Channel, it is also in line with the many maritime pieces produced in France between *La Mer* by Debussy (1905) and *L'Esquisse maritime* by Antoine Mariotte (1932) and *Marine* by Emmanuel Bondeville (1933). Played at least eighteen times until April 1938, the *Pastorale maritimo* was composed (completed?) in 1933 in Varengeville-sur-Mer.[203] According to Heidenreich and Holečková-Heidenreichová, its premiere took place in Belgrade in 1933 (around September 17?), but no other evidence has been found to date.[204] The soprano Alice Raveau included it as an addition to the program of her Scandinavian tour with the Copenhagen Philharmonic Orchestra in February to March 1934.[205] The piece was performed again twice in 1934, first in Prague on April 29 under the direction of Pavel Dědeček,[206] and in Copenhagen on June 6, and then broadcast on Radio-Wien on May 27, 1935, under the baton of Josef Holzer.[207] Yet, it was with the enthusiastic – and apparently encored – performance of this orchestral work at the Vichy Congress on September 4, 1935, that Reisserová succeeded in winning over the critics and establishing herself on the European musical scene. The work, dedicated "To Madame Albert Roussel" ("À Madame Albert Roussel," Blanche Preisach), was immediately given again in Bratislava by the Radio Orchestra and Adolf Heller on November 18 and December 10, 1935, and in Vienna on March 15, 1936, by the Wiener Symphoniker conducted by Bruno Pleier.[208] The *Pastorale maritimo* also seems to be the only piece by Reisserová to have been played in Hungary. In France, the piece was not first programmed in Paris, but in Nancy as part of the Concerts du Conservatoire. Alfred Bachelet, who succeeded Joseph-Guy Ropartz as director of the Conservatoire in 1919, and the Czech artist must have gotten acquainted during their stay in Vichy. Bachelet included the *Pastorale maritimo* in the concert of Sunday February 16, 1936, given in the Salle Victor Poirel, alongside *La Légende de Sonia* from his own musical drama *Quand la cloche sonnera*,

---

[203] In 1931, Reisserová said that she was working on an orchestral piece: Was it the *Pastorale*? See Závada, "Skladatelka Julie Reisserová o sobě," 45.
[204] Heidenreich, "Za Julií Reisserovou," 94; Holečková-Heidenreichová, "Za Julií Reisserovou," 62 and 80; Vacková, *Julie Reisserová*, 61 (no. 4).
[205] *Národní listy večerník* (April 7, 1934), 3; *Národní politika* (April 7, 1934), 8.
[206] *Prager Presse* (April 29, 1934), 5 (photograph of Reisserová); *Večer* (April 25, 1934), 1.
[207] *Innsbrucker Nachrichten* (May 24, 1935), 7.
[208] *Antena* (November 17, 1935), xii; *Antena* (December 8, 1935), xvi (according to Vacková, *Julie Reisserová*, 55, the concert took place on December 16); *Der Wiener Tag* (March 9, 1936), 6; *Kleine Volks-Zeitung* (March 9, 1936), 9; *Salzburger Chronik* (March 14, 1936), 13.

excerpts of which had been heard in the spa town. The local press did not fail to insist on the fact that the *Pastorale* had "obtained a great success at the last international music festival in Vichy."[209] The next day, the critic of *L'Est républicain* recognized that:

> [la] *Pastorale Maritimo*, de Mme Julie Reisserovà [*sic*], est une page fort évocatrice. L'auteur décrit une impression poétique dans un langage de grande distinction. L'ambiance est créée par une instrumentation qui recherche la finesse et la simplicité; elle emploie le glissando des harpes et les trilles des bois pour soutenir le chant vibrant des cordes. L'impression est fort séduisante. Elle fait honneur au métier et à l'inspiration.[210]

> [the] *Pastorale Maritimo*, by Mrs. Julie Reisserová, is a very evocative piece. The author describes a poetic impression in a language of great distinction. The atmosphere is created by an instrumentation that seeks finesse and simplicity; it uses the glissando of the harps and the trills of the woodwinds to support the vibrant singing of the strings. The impression is very seductive. It honors the profession and the inspiration.

The columnist of *L'Éclair de l'Est* was "struck by the clarity of [the composer's] writing. Harmonious phrases, very simple, which seek expression, find it easily and evoke a certain poetry. One listens to them with pleasure and without any fatigue."[211] Given this success, Charles Munch decided to program the work at the concert of the Orchestre de la Société Philharmonique de Paris on Saturday January 28, 1937, at the Salle Pleyel (Figure 5). The overall impression of this first Parisian performance was generally positive. For Paul Dambly, "There is a lot of charm in the fluidity, the transparency, in this mobility of impressions that compose the *Pastorale maritime* of Mrs. Reisserova."[212] René Dumesnil deemed the work "luminous like a seascape, with a colorful but transparent orchestration, and which reveals at the same time an original temperament and a solid craft."[213] For the journalist of the *Excelsior*, the author of the *Pastorale*

---

[209] *L'Est républicain* (February 15, 1936), 4: "Cette œuvre a obtenu un grand succès au dernier festival de musique internationale à Vichy."

[210] H. H., "8ᵉ Concert du Conservatoire," *L'Est républicain* (February 17, 1936), 3. See also *Le Guide du Concert* (January 22, 1937), 432.

[211] Mi Bémol, "Le 8ᵉ concert du Conservatoire," *L'Éclair de l'Est* (February 19, 1936), 3: "j'ai été frappé de la clarté de son écriture. Des phrases harmonieuses, très simples, qui cherchent l'expression, la trouvent facilement et évoquent certaine poésie. On les écoute avec plaisir et sans aucune fatigue." The latter comment is paraphrased by the correspondant of the *Národní listy* (March 13, 1936), 5. See also *Lidové noviny* (February 29, 1936), 9.

[212] Paul Dambly, "Premières auditions symphoniques," *Le Petit journal* (February 1, 1937), 5: "Il y a beaucoup de charme dans la fluidité, la transparence, dans cette mobilité d'impressions qui composent la *Pastorale maritime* de Mme Reisserova."

[213] René Dumesnil, "Musique," *Mercure de France: Série moderne*, CCLXXIV, 48th year, no. 930 (March 15, 1937), 616: "œuvre lumineuse comme un paysage marin, d'une orchestration colorée mais transparente, et qui révèle à la fois un tempérament original et un métier solide."

"cultivates the kind [and] tasty genre, with a perfect happiness."[214] Robert Brussel described it as "delicate and expressive."[215] Hélène Jourdan-Morhange saw in it "a pretty 'pastel' with fresh and young colors" evoking Roussel.[216] The correspondent of the *Národní listy* hailed the rich and refined nuances of a score warmly received by the public,[217] J. M. Pellé was transported to "a real realm of delicate poetry,"[218] and Edmund J. Pendleton enjoyed its "gentl[e] seductive lines."[219] In Germany, Eduard Levi praised "a new seascape on the theme 'Meeresstille und glückliche Fahrt,'" and the idyllic atmosphere of the score.[220] On the other hand, for the critic of the magazine *Commune*, the *Pastorale maritimo* "is very pleasant, but its composition does not seem to have been imposed by an inescapable impulse of inspiration,"[221] while for Denyse Bertrand, it "evokes nature without aggressiveness as well as without brilliance, [and] hardly escapes from the beaten paths."[222] This mixed opinion was also that of Louis-Charles Bérard (*alias* Carol-Bérard) for whom "the *Pastorale maritime* of Mrs. Reis[s]erova could not pretend to have any other purpose than to charm us with its skillfully chiseled harmonies."[223] Among the reviews published after the Paris premiere, two should be singled out for their gendered and somewhat misogynistic language. André Cœuroy caustically stated that the Parisian public found Julie Reisserová "too pretty" ("trop jolie") in her *Pastorale*.[224] Irwing Schwerké praised the quality of the music while softening his compliment with a touch of condescending humor:

---

[214] Pierre Leroi, "Concert de l'Orchestre de la Société Philharmonique," *Excelsior* (January 31, 1937), 7: "[Reisserová] cultive le genre aimable, savoureux, avec un bonheur parfait."
[215] Robert Brussel, "Chronique des concerts," *Le Figaro* (February 15, 1937), 4: "délicate et expressive."
[216] Hélène Jourdan-Morhange, "Charles Munch et l'orchestre philharmonique," *La République* (February 2, 1937), 6: "Un jolie 'pastel' aux couleurs fraîches et jeunes."
[217] *Národní listy* (January 30, 1937), 2.
[218] J. M. Pellé, "Julie Reisserová v Paříži," 5: "skutečné říše jemné poesie."
[219] Edmund J. Pendleton, "Françaix's 'La Lutherie Enchantée' to Have Paris Premiere Tomorrow," *New York Herald Tribune* (January 30, 1937), 5.
[220] Eduard Levi, "Neue Musik," *Pariser Tageszeitung*, 245 (February 11, 1937), 4 : "eine neue Marine über das Thema etwa: 'Meeresstille und glückliche Fahrt.'"
[221] *Commune: Revue littéraire française pour la défense de la culture*, 43–47 (1937), 877: the *Pastorale* "est fort aimable, mais sa composition ne semble pas avoir été imposée par un inéluctable élan d'inspiration." André George shared the same feeling in *Les Nouvelles littéraires, artistiques et scientifiques* (February 13, 1937), [10].
[222] Denyse Bertrand, "Société Philharmonique de Paris," *Le Ménestrel*, 99th year, no. 6 (February 5, 1937), 47: "[Reisserová] évoqu[e] la nature sans agressivité comme sans éclat, ne s'évade guère des sentiers battus."
[223] Carol-Bérard, "Les récitals," *L'Écho de Paris* (February 3, 1937), 4: "la *Pastorale maritime* de Mme Reis[s]erova ne saurait prétendre à d'autres fins qu'à nous charmer par ses harmonies adroitement ciselées."
[224] André Cœuroy, "Atmosphère de bagarre," *Beaux-Arts* (February 5, 1937), 7.

The Eternal Feminine.

... I am very fond of the company of ladies: I like their beauty, their delicacy, their vivacity, and sometimes I like – their music. The Philharmonic concert was one of those times. It brought us a cleverly worked-out and intimate sounding "Pastorale Maritime" by Julie Reisserova, from Czecho-Slovakia. The piece would seem to have all the elements essential to success. An evocation of nature, to which so many people are trying to get back, its harmonious phrases, limpid orchestration, and vibrant singing in the strings, are productive of a welcome, fresh-air atmosphere.[225]

To sum up, the *Pastorale maritimo*, qualified as a "symphonic poem"[226] by a Swiss critic, was favorably received by the majority of commentators, and was the most discussed piece by the composer during her lifetime. Only four critics were more reserved – and more impartial? – about it, those of *Le Ménestrel*, *L'Écho de Paris*, the *Commune*, and *Les Nouvelles littéraires* which denounced a certain lack of originality. Following the Parisian premiere, the piece was broadcast on Radio-Strasbourg on March 19, 1937.

4.5 Pod sněhem

The song cycle with piano *Pod sněhem* [*Sous la neige*] (*Under the Snow*) is said to be Reisserová's last completed work and, according to Vacková, was composed in 1937.[227] However, the advertising insert printed at the end of the vocal score of *Březen* (1934) leads one to believe that a manuscript copy was available as early as 1934, or at least was announced as such. What is more, the words "klav[írní]. výtah" on the title page of the only known source suggest that the latter might be a piano reduction of a version with orchestral accompaniment, of which there is no trace or mention in the surviving documents. *Pod sněhem* gathers three songs on Chinese verses in a French adaptation by Franz Toussaint published in *La Flûte de Jade*.[228] These are dedicated to three famous female singers: *Vzpomínka* [*Souvenir*; *Erinnerung*] (*Recollection*) to Inger Raasløff, *Bílá volavka* [*Le Héron blanc*; *Der weisse Reiher*] (*The White Heron*) to Elšlégravá Puklová, and *Příznivá bouřka* [*L'Orage favorable*; *Das gute Unwetter*] (*The Favorable Storm*) to Else Schøtt. Reisserová's poetic choices do not seem insignificant; they respond to the interest – widespread in Europe at the beginning of the twentieth century – for Chinese culture.[229] *La Flûte de Jade*

---

[225] Irving Schwerké, "Paris," *The Musical Times*, 78 (February 1937), 171.
[226] *Der Bund* (March 17, 1938), 3: "symphonische Dichtung."
[227] Vacková, *Julie Reisserová*, 23.
[228] Franz Toussaint, *La Flûte de Jade: Poésies chinoises* (Paris: L'édition d'art H. Piazza, 1920), 31, 33–34, 52–53.
[229] Roussel set six Chinese poems to music between 1907 and 1932 (op. 12, 35, and 47). Alfred Henschke authored a German version of *Bílá volavka* that was popular with composers.

Figure 5 From left to right: Albert Roussel, Julie Reisserová, and Charles Munch in Paris, 1937.
Image courtesy of the Moravian Library in Brno; call-number: Gr1-1251.622. Originally published in *Prager Presse* (February 7, 1937), 4; *Pestrý týden* (February 13, 1937), 5.

was a popular collection that provided words for many *mélodies*, such as those of Armande de Polignac (1922), Marguerite Canal (1922), Raymond Moulaert (1922), and Jean Cartan (1928), sung in the interwar period.[230] Hence, the poems of *Pod sněhem* were also set to music by Cartan, Moulaert, and Polignac. Unlike *Březen*, *Pod sněhem* is about the coldness and stillness of winter, and then – as a counterpart to *Jaro v ulici* – the eroticized arrival of the beloved (*Příznivá bouřka*).

---

[230] Hamer, *Female Composers*, 64, 86.

The cycle was most probably given for the first time in public by Gilberte Arvez-Vernet, accompanied by Aline van Bärentzen, on September 11, 1936, at the Social Club (Společenský klub) in Prague alongside the celebrations of the Interallied Federation of Veterans (Fédération Interalliée Des Anciens Combattants) partly organized by the FIDAC Women's Union,[231] then by various female singers (such as Raasløff), sometimes with the composer herself on the piano.

4.6 Slavnostní den

Slavnostní den (*Festive Day*) for female chorus, composed to a poem by Reisserová at Varengeville-sur-Mer, was – according to the published score – completed on September 24, 1935, to celebrate the sixtieth birthday of Františka Plamínková. Naturally dedicated to the latter, the work was publicly premiered in Prague on December 3, 1937, by members of the Singing Association of Prague Female Teachers and performed again in Philadelphia in January 1938 by Sophie Drinker's female choir, the Montgomery Singers, probably under the direction of Lela Vauclain.[232] The piece was also sung in Prague on April 26, 1938, and in 1948 by the Philharmonic Choir of Brno.[233] *Slavnostní den*, the reception of which is unknown, depicts the joy and exultation of a group of young girls at the arrival of the sweet and magical month of May (a month rich in popular traditions). *Slavnostní den* is Reisserová's third known choir after *Dva mužské sbory* (*Two Male Choirs*), which she probably penned in Bern in 1929, following her choral conducting lessons.

4.7 Předjaří

Předjaří [*Février*; *Februar*; *Vorfrühling*] (*Early Spring*) is the first of three songs that were to constitute a cycle for coloratura soprano and orchestra. The lyrics by the Swiss poet Werner Rudolf Beer were translated into French by René Chalupt, a friend of Roussel, and probably by Reisserová into Czech.[234] It greets the coming of spring and the birth of a little fly that will take flight and go far away. This piece, composed in 1936, is dedicated to the soprano Maria Jensen-Milliet, who sang the work for the

---

[231] *Národní politika* (September 6, 1936), 5; *Národní listy* (September 11, 1936), 2; *Prager Presse* (September 9, 1936), 5; *Prager Presse* (September 11, 1936), 5.

[232] *Národní politika* (February 1, 1938), 7.

[233] Antonín Kolář (ed.), *Sto let Filharmonického sboru Besedy Brněnské* (Brno: Krajské nakladatelství, 1960), 78, 99.

[234] Roussel, who set several of René Chalupt's poems to music, may have played the intermediary between Reisserová and the writer. On Chalupt and Roussel, see Catherine Miller, "René Chalupt (1885–1957), poète et critique, et Albert Roussel (1869–1937), compositeur," *Lettres romanes*, vol. 53, nos. 1–2 (1999), 109–125.

first time on January 13, 1937, in Zurich, accompanied on the piano by Hedi Durrer.[235] It was sung again by O. Guerfort (with Mrs. Blanchard de Chatillon at the piano) during the concert held in Paris on April 28, 1938. No other performance is documented, and it cannot be ascertained whether the orchestral version – if it ever existed – was presented to the public. The sources of this *mélodie*, which likely remained in the possession of Jan Reisser after the death of his wife, are lost,[236] as are those used by the musicians for the Parisian concert just mentioned. According to Élisabeth de Mondésir the song was a "page remarkable for its sonic exuberance and melodic richness."[237]

4.8 Sources and Public Performances

Only two works found their way to the press and are fairly easily accessible: the piano-vocal version of *Březen* due to Emil Hájek and the *Esquisses* were issued in Copenhagen by Skandinavisk og borups Verlag in 1934 and 1935 respectively.[238] The orchestral works – *Suita, Pastorale maritimo*, and the symphonic version of *Březen* – as well as *Slavnostní den* were not officially published, but circulated confidentially in a photostatic edition prepared around 1934–1935 by the Atelier Elektra, a workshop located in Copenhagen (Kompagnistræde 22) and founded in 1900 by Aage Højring. These photostatic editions are available at the Royal Danish Library and at the Library of the Conservatoire régional du Grand-Nancy (France); the latter library also holds the autograph manuscript of the *Pastorale maritimo* (Figure 6; Appendix B). It is not clear how this autograph arrived in Nancy. It is possible – but very doubtful – that Reisserová attended the Nancy concert of the *Pastorale* and gave it to Bachelet. It can also be surmised that the autograph score was either handed over in Vichy, or passed on by a certain G. Roché to whom the composer dedicated one of the two printed copies of *Březen* (which contains some handwritten corrections) now preserved in Nancy along with a signed copy of the *Esquisses*.[239]

---

[235] *Neue Zürcher Nachrichten* (January 13, 1937), 3; *Neue Zürcher Zeitung*, Blatt 2 (January 18, 1937), [5]; *Národní listy* (January 18, 1937), 2.

[236] The Czech translation of the poem, a facsimile reproduction of the first page of a manuscript copy, and a description of the score are available in Vacková, *Julie Reisserová*, 3 and 21–23.

[237] Mondésir, "Hommage à J. Reisserova," 781: "page remarquable par son exubérance sonore et sa richesse mélodique."

[238] From the advertisement inserted in the prints of *Březen* and *Esquisses*, the orchestral score of *Březen* appears to have been published by the Danish company as well, but no copies have been found.

[239] *Březen*, Library of the Conservatoire régional du Grand-Nancy, call-number 511.1 REI: "A mes chers amis G. Roché / bien sincèrement / [signature] Julie Reisserové / Copenhague Noël

Figure 6 First Page of the Autograph Manuscript of the *Pastorale maritimo*. Image Courtesy of the Library of the Conservatoire régional du Grand-Nancy; no call-number.

1934." *Esquisses*, call-number 111 REI. See also note 78. The dedicatee may be Georges Albert Roché (1866–1942), doctor of natural sciences, perpetual member of the board of directors of the Union of Chemical Industries and general inspector of maritime fisheries. See Montagnier (ed.), *Reisserová: Musique de chambre*, 64–65; Montagnier, "Autour de la *Pastorale maritimo*," 155.

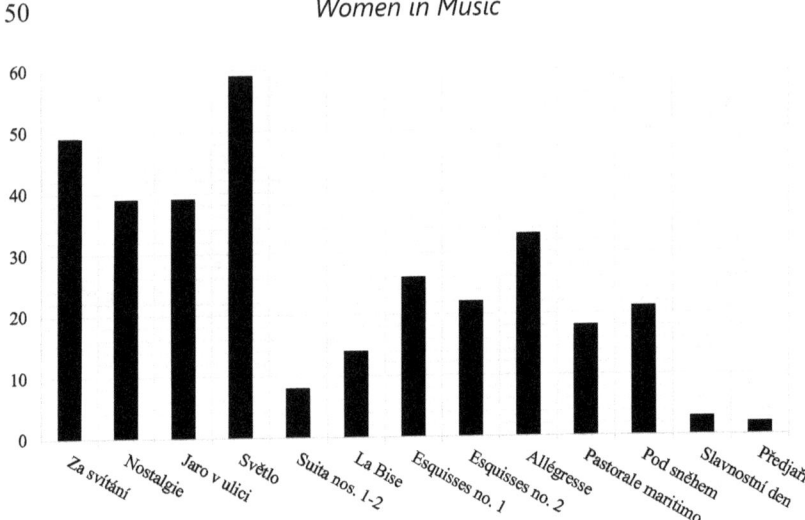

Figure 7 Documented number of public and radio performances between 1927 and 1941 (Appendix C). Newspapers allude to other performances without providing usable data.

Pod sněhem has come down to us in a non-autograph manuscript deposited in the Women Composers Collection of the University of Michigan Music Library. As for the sources of *Předjaří*, as already said, they disappeared following the February 1948 coup d'état and Jan Reisser's decision to settle permanently in Brazil to escape the communist regime. Thus, our knowledge of the work is based only on Vacková's description and her facsimile of the first page of an unidentified handwritten copy.[240]

Reisserová's seven completed scores were heard a creditable number of times (Figure 7), which is noteworthy for a composer who did not devote all her time to composition, and who – as she used to say – did not want to be a "curiosity" ("kuriosit[a]").[241] This latter claim may not imply that she had no interest in self-promotion, as it is possible that she declared this – deliberately or not – to emphasize her productivity and to position herself compared to male contemporaries. Besides, the fact that her new scores were regularly announced in *Rytmus* and *Tempo* testifies to her interest in promoting her work.[242] The *Březen* songs (notably in their piano-vocal version) and *Allégresse* were unsurprisingly

---

[240] For an edition of the scores and a description of the sources, see Jean-Paul C. Montagnier (ed.), *Reisserová: Œuvres pour orchestre/Orchestral Works* (Berlin: Ries & Erler, 2022); *Reisserová: Březen. Version avec orchestre/Orchestral Version* (Berlin: Ries & Erler, 2023); and *Reisserová: Musique de chambre*.

[241] Vacková, *Julie Reisserová*, 8.

[242] *Rytmus* I (1935–1936), 67; *Rytmus* IV (1938–1939), 8. *Tempo* XV (1935–1936), 95, 131; *Tempo* XVI (1936–1937), 38, 139.

the most frequently performed in public, as they were the first pieces to be composed and their printed scores facilitated their dissemination. The orchestral works being more difficult and expensive to program, *La Bise* and the *Pastorale maritimo* were played a dozen times or so. Moreover, this body of work attracted the greatest artists of the period, a detail which speaks in favor of its quality.

4.9 Poems

Besides composing, Reisserová enjoyed attending theatrical performances and playing with words. She had a facility to learn foreign languages and mastered not only French and English, but also German,[243] which she practiced at home as a child. Thus, she translated – or rather adapted – into Czech, German poems by Gustav Falke and Heinrich Heine respectively set to music by Foerster in his *Noční violy*, op. 43 (1913), and Jirák in his *Lyrické Intermezzo*, op. 4 (1925).[244] While attending the Music Club, she collaborated with her brother in the translation of the librettos of *Der Ring des Nibelungen* and of *Parsifal*.[245] Similarly, for the premiere of Roussel's *Le Testament de la tante Caroline*, she translated into Czech the libretto by Nino (Michel Veber). She also supplied the French, German, and Czech versions of all the lyrics of her song cycles.

Ever since childhood, she could write with ease poems, epigrams, verses, and all kind of fables: lyric, epic, witty, serious. She made a selection of them in 1934 under the title *In margine vitæ*. Since the autograph copy of the latter disappeared after her death, we have to rely on Vacková's description of the collection. It gathered texts in Czech, German, French, and English, distributed into two sections, one subjective and the other objective. "At Home" ("Doma") dealt with her inner experience before her marriage; it addressed topics like love, wisdom about life, bitter experiences, and social and religious feelings. "Years Abroad" ("Léta v cizině") described her longing for home, her love for Czech nature, and her impressions of the capitals in which she stayed.[246] This second section likely echoed the Andantino espressivo of the *Suita* that depicts "an expression of memories and homesickness, which I do not have time to indulge in at length." Out of the several hundreds of texts she produced, only

---

[243] She enjoyed reading Schiller and Goethe.
[244] Josef Bohuslav Foerster, *Nachtviolen: Vier Lieder aus dem Zyklus "Eine Liebe" von Gustav Falke . . . Noční violy* (Vienna, Leipzig: Universal Edition, 1913); Karel Boleslav Jirák, *Lyrické intermezzo: Cyklus písní. . . na slova H. Heineho z "Knihy písní"; přeložila Julie Kühnlová* (Prague: Fr. Chadím, n.d.). When she undertook these translations, she was not yet Foerster's pupil nor yet married, hence the use of her maiden name (Vacková, *Julie Reisserová*, 8).
[245] Čornej, *Historici, historiografie a dějepis*, 289.
[246] Vacková, *Julie Reisserová*, 11. The author records the titles of two other poems: *Soucit* (*Compassion*), and *Děti z předměstí* (*Children from the Suburbs*). See also Vacková, "Hudební tvorba Julie Reisserové," [3].

four survive (titles are given in their original language): *Das Licht* (ca. 1923) and *Printemps dans la rue* (1925) included in *Březen, Slavnostní den* set to music in 1935, and *Mé myšlení* (*My Thinking*) which Vacková reproduced in her book. The latter sees it as the manifestation of Reisserová's lack of confidence in her creative work.[247] Yet, the poem could also be read as an expression of women's efforts to assert themselves in a man's world. All her life, the composer indeed plowed her musical land slowly and with much self-censorship:

> *Mé myšlení*
> Já rvu se, zápasím o každou píd' –
> tak za krokem krok
> co jiní vzdušnou spirálou ptáka se vznesou nad světy –
> Své pole na svahu vryté
> zorávám rok co rok –
> úzkostí, modlitbou v neklidných nocích
> co jiným v zraky krásou zpité
> rozkvetlý luh plá barvou v ústrety.

> *My Thinking* I fight, I struggle for every span – step by step as others soar over the worlds in the airy spiral of a bird – I plow my field carved on the slope year after year – with anguish, with prayer in restless nights as the flowery meadow blazes with color to meet others gazing at the beauty.

Reisserová's poetic muse usually announced her musical inspiration, and led her to say: "I'm getting verses in my pen again. I'll be composing soon."[248] Music and poetry were therefore tightly connected in her creative process.

Seen from the outside, Reisserová's music shares some characteristics of Smetana's output, whom Janáček questionably considered to represent "Czechness" in music: a love of nature, as evidenced by some titles of her scores and the contents of the poems she set to music, and an interest in everyday events, such as the *Suita*, which was inspired by the personal life of its composer, not to mention her love for her country.[249]

5 Stylistic Considerations

In her introduction to the tribute concert given in Prague in 1940, and during which Roussel's trio for flute, viola, and cello, op. 40, was programmed, Jiřina Vacková was accused of "perhaps overestimating the importance of [Reisserová,] this otherwise quite unique phenomenon." While the *Národní politika* journalist

---

[247] Vacková, *Julie Reisserová*, 12.
[248] Vacková, *Julie Reisserová*, 11: "Už se mi zase derou verše do pera. To už budu brzy komponovat."
[249] Michael Beckerman, "In Search of Czechness in Music," *19th-Century Music*, vol. 10, no. 1 (Summer, 1986), 66.

conceded that the composer had a personality, he denied the individuality of her music, as it is eclectic, and combines "so many styles ... that there can be no question of a personality in any sense of the word."[250] Instinctively, the reporter could not help comparing Reisserová's music with that of her master Roussel. But what seems to have disappointed him was welcomed by the French audience. As the anonymous contributor of *La Revue musicale* put it: "the influence of the master is evident in her style, but this is not to our displeasure ... we still find in [her work] the most sympathetic concern to deviate from the beaten track and to express herself in a personal and new language."[251] The question is therefore to define her musical style. To do this, scores need to be scrutinized while keeping an eye on contemporary reviews.

5.1 Influences and Similarities

Reisserová's musical pantheon was diverse – Dvořák, Mahler, Mozart (*Le nozze di Figaro* was her favorite opera), Ravel, Rimski-Korsakov (notably his *Capriccio espagnol*), Roussel, Smetana, Richard Strauss (she enjoyed *Salome* and *Der Rosenkavalier*), Wagner[252] – but not all of them had an effect on her style. Like most if not all composers, she was unconsciously influenced by the music she had played or heard. Thus, some pianistic figurations in the *Esquisses* may call to mind Chopin's *Études* and Bach's two- and four-voice counterpoint, while the symphonic prelude to *Nostalgie* and *Za svítání* may respectively be a reminder of the beginning of the Moon Song and "Rusalko, znáš mne, znáš?" (Act II) from Dvořák's *Rusalka*. Likewise, Mahler hovers above the final cadences of *Za svítání* (mm. 72–76) and *Nostalgie* (mm. 41–42). Vacková, whose hidden purpose was perhaps to prove that her heroine did "not deny her Slavic origin,"[253] noticed similarities between the *Esquisses* no. 3 and Novak's *Píseň noci karnevalové*, op. 30 no. 4, and between the string accompaniment in measures one to nineteen of *La Bise* (*Suita* no. 3) and the opening measures of Smetana's *Vltava* (*The Moldau*). She even went as far as to connect the four-note cell ($d\flat$-c-$g\flat$-$b\flat$) of the *Esquisses* no. 2 (mm. 84–85) to the fugue subject of Novak's string quartet, op. 35. She then compared – not without reason – the

---

[250] *Národní politika* (February 25, 1940), 8: "snad přece jen preceňujíci význam tohoto jinak doci ojedinělého zjevu ... spojuje v několika skladbách tolik slohů, že o osobnosti v jediném slova smyslu nemůže býti ani řeči."

[251] "Les mardis de la Revue musicale," *La Revue musicale*, vol. 18, no. 172 (February–March, 1937), 151: "l'influence du maître transparaît dans son style, mais ce n'est point pour nous déplaire.... on y trouve encore le plus sympathique souci de s'écarter des sentiers battus et de s'exprimer dans une langue personnelle et neuve."

[252] After Jan Reisser, *Léta s Julkou*, quoted in Vacková, *Julie Reisserová*, 7.

[253] Vacková, *Julie Reisserová*, 47: "Ve své tvorbě nezapře Julie Reisserová ani svůj slovanský původ."

chromatic beginning of *Nostalgie* and the use of the English horn to Wagner's *Tristan und Isolde* (did she allude to the prelude to Act III?). Finally, her comparison between the 3/4 section of the *Pastorale maritimo* (mm. 39–42) and the fourth piece ("***. Andante") of Josef Suk's *Jaro*, op. 22a, sounds convincing.[254] In both scores, the same melodic motif – a descending major second followed by a fourth and a minor second – is punctuated by an ascending arpeggio (Example 1). Still, it cannot be ruled out that this resemblance is the result of an unconscious coincidence. In any event, this kind of similitude may be the reason that prompted André Chastain to assert (about the *Pastorale maritimo* in particular?) that "Mrs. Reisserová drew on specifically Slavic sources of inspiration. Even though she did not try to transpose or harmonize popular music motifs, she found in a national repertoire admirable themes, the rudimentary frameworks of her learned and harmonious compositions."[255]

To the composers of influence already mentioned, at least two others should be added: Stravinsky, whose mechanical rhythms found a distant echo in *Jaro v ulici*, and Scriabin, whose style, according to the chronicler of the *Neue Zürcher Zeitung*, would permeate the *Esquisses* no. 1. The same commentator also considered that *Světlo* and *Předjaří* leaned "toward early impressionism."[256] From these samples and the reviews already cited earlier in this Element, it appears that Reisserová was receptive to the musical

Example 1a Josef Suk, *Jaro* [*Spring*], op. 22a, "***. Andante," mm. 1–6.

---

[254] Vacková, *Julie Reisserová*, 42.
[255] André Chastain, "Une compositrice tchèque: Mme Julie Reisserova au Festival de Vichy," *Comœdia* (September 13, 1935), 5: "Mme Reisserova a puisé à des sources d'inspiration spécifiquement slaves. Encore qu'elle n'ait point cherché à transposer, à harmoniser des motifs de musique populaire, elle a trouvé dans un répertoire national des thèmes admirables, les trames rudimentaires de ses savantes et harmonieuses compositions."
[256] *Neue Zürcher Zeitung*, Blatt 2 (January 18, 1937), [5]: "... zwei dem frühern Impressionismus zuneigende Lieder..."

Example 1b Julie Reisserová, *Pastorale maritimo*, mm. 39–44 (horn and timpani omitted).

world around her and was able to digest new trends to express herself through sound.

Nonetheless, Roussel remained the one who had a decisive impact on her musical expression.[257] The melody in Example 1b – which is distinguished by its large leaps, a gesture often found in Roussel's melodic writing – can also be compared to the first theme of his Fourth Symphony, op. 53 (Example 2). This detail allows us to surmise that since Reisserová worked on her *Pastorale* in

---

[257] *Národní listy* (October 31, 1931), 4.

Example 2 Albert Roussel, Fourth Symphony, op. 53, first movement, mm. 18–21.

Varengeville-sur-Mer while Roussel was composing his symphony, they probably discussed their scores in progress.

Reisserová's musical dependence on Roussel is particularly evident in her orchestral music, mainly in the Allegro giocoso and the Andante espressivo of the *Suita*, as well as in the *Pastorale maritimo*. Several obvious common features can be detected. Both composers have a taste for irresistible rhythmic impulses, as evidenced by the opening measures of the Allegro giocoso, which have the same impetus as the beginning of the Third Symphony, op. 42, and the introduction to *Bacchus et Ariane*, op. 43. Both share ample and well-chiseled melodies, characterized by a variety of rhythms, sometimes irregular, as shown in Example 1b. Both use a fluid and sometimes chromatic harmonic vocabulary, a tight counterpoint, and light French orchestration. On this last point, a mere comparison of the first two movements of the *Suita* and the *Pastorale maritimo* with *La Bise* and, to a lesser extent, *Březen* is revealing: the former bring out individual timbres (see Example 5 in 5.3), whereas the latter – scored under Hohlfeld's supervision – require heavy instrumental doublings.[258]

5.2 Form

Because of the conciseness of Reisserová's scores, and in spite of her own statement that in the process of composing "the bubbling source of ideas [ought to be] put into a form that makes the ideas comprehensible to the outside world,"[259] form does not seem to have been her main concern. The structure of each song logically follows the poetic content of the poem. For instance, *Bílá volavka* is a short, gloomy arioso of unitary form. Conversely, *Za svítání* counts three sections: A (Impetuoso, mm. 1–33), in E flat minor, renders the narrator's troubled mind and doubts through a sixteenth-note ostinato; B (Andante espressivo, cantabile, mm. 34–50), revolving around G flat major, depicts the recovery of inner calm through a continuum of triplets and an accompaniment provided primarily by the string quintet; C (Andante, mm. 51–63) is a short lullaby in A major that greets the sunrise and the morning bells; a symphonic conclusion

---

[258] The instrumentation of *Březen* is favorably described in *Lidové noviny* (September 15, 1936), 9.
[259] See Appendix A.

(mm. 62–76) in D minor, which returns to the hectic atmosphere of A, and at the last moment (mm. 72–76) to the calm of B, brings the piece to an end. The chaotic tonal progression in two sequences spaced an augmented second apart is noteworthy and parallels the evolution of the narrator's feelings: E flat minor/G flat major; A major/D minor. As for her instrumental music, it conforms principally to the ternary form ABA' (rounded off by a brief introduction and/or conclusion), or to its cognate ABA'B'A" in the *Pastorale maritimo*. The first movement of the *Suita* must be singled out, as it betrays the influence of Roussel's fondness for arch forms: section A introduces three fragments *a* (mm. 1–3), *b* (mm. 4–11) and *c* (mm. 12–20) which are recapitulated in an almost inverted order (*b*, *c*, and *a*).

Conversely, the forms of the *Esquisses* nos. 1 and 3, and that of *La Bise* are far from clear. In fact, these pieces are best described as a mosaic of short motifs – if not cells – intertwined with each other and developed alternately, but always with ease and fluidity. In this regard, these pieces might reflect Reisserová's art of improvisation. For instance, in the *Esquisses* no. 1, cell *a* establishes the key of A minor through a strong dominant-tonic progression and a strong "Czech-like" first-beat accent, and is followed by at least five further sharply defined units that are expanded in the course of the piece: a chromatic ascent (*b*), a succession of accented chords (*c*), a light and airy motif in triplets (*d*), a descending pentatonic arpeggio (*e*), and a circular bitonal cell (*f*) in which the dominant and tonic chords of F sharp minor are combined (Example 3).

Similarly, *La Bise* unfolds an endless flow – the north wind on Lake Geneva – derived from a four-measure motif (mm. 3–6) that is restated by augmentation toward the end of the piece (mm. 66–69), and a flow briefly interrupted by a stormy motif (mm. 20–25). This formal freedom, comparable to that of the *Esquisses* nos. 1 and 3, is due to the narrative character of the music, even though there is no extant literary program for the latter two pieces.

5.3 Harmony and Counterpoint

Reisserová did not stray far from tonality in her music. If chromatic progressions of neoromantic type are not rare (especially in *Světlo*, *Nostalgie*, *Esquisses* no. 2, and *La Bise*) and can be contrasted with pure diatonic episodes (as it is the case in *Za svítání*), she was nevertheless sensitive to modal colors, such as the "Gypsy" scale on G (an Aeolian mode with the fourth degree augmented: g, a, b♭, c♯, d, e♭, f) at the beginning of *Vzpomínka*,[260] and pentatonic scales

---

[260] The instrumental accompaniment at the beginning of *Předjaří* (mm. 1–7) evokes that of *Vzpomínka*, both melodically and harmonically, with a kind of superposition of the key of D flat major (right hand) with that of its relative B flat minor (left hand; ascending melodic minor scale); see Montagnier (ed.), *Julie Reisserová: Musique de chambre/Chamber Music*, [70].

Example 3 Julie Reisserová, *Esquisses* no. 1: (a) m. 1; (b) m. 3; (c) m. 12; (d) m. 26; (e) m. 30; (f) m. 35.

(*Esquisses* no. 1, mm. 30–31, 40–41, 50–53).[261] She also assimilated characteristics prevalent in France and in Roussel's music in particular. Thus, *Bílá volavka* stands alone in her entire output for its remarkably rich and dissonant harmonic vocabulary. Yet, a careful analysis shows that the dissonant chords – which are the "symbol of the majesty of death" (Reisserová *dixit*)[262] – are caused by the superimposition of various non-chordal tones, and notably of unresolved appoggiaturas. This technique was often used by Roussel from 1921 onward. Therefore, in spite of its dissonances, *Bílá volavka* is deeply rooted in D flat major (as is clarified by the tonic and dominant pedals in the bass, and the alternation of the fundamentals I, V, and II), and its first phrase goes effortlessly from the home key to that of G flat major (Example 4).

Most of the time, Reisserová's harmony oscillates gently between minor and major colors and includes many altered and unaltered seventh and ninth chords. The *Pastorale maritimo*, *Za svítání*, *Nostalgie*, *Vzpomínka*, *Příznivá bouřka*, and *Slavnostní den* begin in one tonality and end in another, either in the relative

---

[261] Roussel was reknown for using a wide variety of modes to enrich his harmonic and melodic vocabulary. He may have passed on some of this taste to his pupil. See Arthur Hoerée, "La technique," *Albert Roussel: Numéro spécial de la Revue musicale* (April 1929), 86–87.

[262] Vacková, *Julie Reisserová*, 24: "symbol majestátu smrti."

Example 4 Julie Reisserová, *Bílá volavka*, mm. 1–12, and harmonic reduction.

key (*Pastorale maritimo*, *Slavnostní den*), on the dominant chord (*Příznivá bouřka*), or even one second apart (*Za svítání*: E flat minor/D minor). The last chord may include an added fourth (*Za svítání*), be a minor ninth chord without the third (*Vzpomínka*: c-g-bb-db), or a stacking of fourths (*Nostalgie*: g-c-f-bb).

Following the lead of Roussel, Reisserová paid great attention to counterpoint and to the melodic quality of her instrumental and/or vocal parts. As she avowed in 1931, "I started my musical career as a singer. The culture of singing is a valuable tool for me even when creating purely orchestral music. In this I follow the old masters a little, but with a difference: they sometimes treat the voice as an instrument, I, on the other hand, strive to treat every instrument as a voice, so that everyone can sing and make it 'fit.'"[263] The *Pastorale maritimo* provides a magnificent sample of melodic and timbral counterpoint. In measures 8–21, a protean melody is articulated in turn by the oboe, flute, and/or violins, and combined with countermelodies in the other parts. The crescendo toward the climax (m. 16), itself underlined by the entrance of the harp, is reached by the doubling of the first violins by the flute and the clarinet, and by the beautiful contrary motion between the upper parts and the bassoon and cellos (Example 5). In the following measures (mm. 22–29), the timbral color of the *Pastorale* becomes even more airy and akin to chamber music: the oboe and bassoon initiate a loose imitative counterpoint on which the clarinet and the horn articulate more or less independent lines, the whole episode being underlined by the strings in pizzicato.

Likewise, *Slavnostní den* for female chorus reveals a nice web of melodic lines that intertwine around the second soprano part. In measures 45–58, the composer notably builds a grand crescendo and swirling dance movement through imitative counterpoint to express the joyful bustle and ardor of youth. Here, Reisserová reminds us that she studied with Roussel, whom Francis Poulenc called a "wonderful teacher of energy."[264]

5.4 Words and Music

The 1931 avowal mentioned in Section 5.3 describes Reisserová's vocal writing, which remains elegant and elastic at all times. High notes are always prepared naturally by an ascending curve, and the melodic line itself avoids large intervals: hence, ascending and descending sixths and sevenths are scarce and reserved for dramatic climaxes, as measures 49–52 of *Jaro v ulici* ("Mais le désir me pousse"; "But desire pushes me") illustrate. The vocal soprano line is mainly syllabic (Example 4), with the possible exception of *Předjaří*, which was designed for a coloratura soprano. In other words, Reisserová is at her best in vocal music. *Březen*, and the first song she wrote in particular (*Světlo*), is pure romantic emotion, while her instrumental scores are less laden with pathos.

The instrumental accompaniment establishes the general atmosphere of the poem and renders its affect. *Příznivá bouřka* provides a nice case in point. In its

---

[263] E. K., "Z rozhovorů s Julii Reisserovou," 4: "Vždyť jsem začínala svou hudební kariéru jako zpěvačka. Kultura zpěvu je mi cennou pomůckou i při tvoření čistě orchestrálním. V tom trochu sleduji staré mistry, ovšem s jistým rozdílem: oni někdy traktují hlas jako nástroj, já zase naopak usiluji o to traktovat každý nástroj jako hlas, aby si každý zazpíval a aby mu to 'leželo.'"

[264] Poulenc cited from Harry Halbreich, "Données de son style," in *Albert Roussel, 1869–1937* (Paris: Actes Sud, École normale supérieure, Sacem, 1987), 39: "magnifique professeur d'énergie."

Example 5 Julie Reisserová, *Pastorale maritimo*, mm. 8–17.

first part (Allegro impetuoso, mm. 1–47), the circular sixteenth-note ostinato depicts the "bad and nasty wind" ("le mauvais et méchant vent") that keeps the lover awake; in the second part (Andante amoroso, mm. 48–75), the vehement ostinato gives way to a still circular motif, but this time gentle, to emphasize the arrival of the beloved and the narrator's growing desire. Similarly, and as shown in Example 4, the dark and morbid mood absent from the poem (*Bílá volavka*) is only suggested by the piano. As for *Nostalgie*, it must be singled out for its symphonic writing. The song begins with an extended orchestral prelude (mm. 1–22) whose fluctuating tempo is paralleled by the variety of the time signatures. The first six chromatic measures, which revolve around D minor and in which the English horn unfolds a beautiful but simple melody, paint the night (i.e., the winter). From the first inversion of the A flat major chord on the downbeat of measure 7, the harmonic color changes and oscillates between E flat major and C minor; the tempo becomes more and more animated; the orchestral texture grows thicker and thicker: the sun is now slowly rising. The stage being set, the voice can naturally utter its first verses: "Already the dark winter night has fled, / Here spring is reborn" ("Déjà la sombre nuit d'hiver a fui, / Voilà que renaît le printemps"). In the following measures, Reisserová relies on the flutes and the quintuplets articulated by the reeds to imitate the "wild bird" ("oiseau sauvage"), on the *tremoli* of the strings to suggest the "silver clouds" ("nues d'argent"), and on the ascending line of the violins and the English horn (mm. 29–30) to render the opening of the bird's wings that should take the narrator to the beloved. The narrator's longing is underlined by the high range of the voice doubled in turn by the oboes and the flutes. The dissonant final chord, delicately played by the strings, the horns, the bassoons, and the oboes, leaves one to think that the young man's wish to be reunited with the person he loves has not yet been fulfilled. Although these imitative musical devices are centuries old, they are judiciously deployed and serve the lyrics effectively.

One last detail is worth noting. Reisserová set four Chinese poems, but contrary to the trend for exoticism at the turn of the century, she never attempted to mimic Far Eastern sonorities by incorporating "distinctive scales, harmonies, orchestral colors, and other features that had previously been associated with exotic realms."[265] None of the *mélodies* in *Pod sněhem* or *Nostalgie* make use of such devices. Neither the "Gypsy" scale of *Vzpomínka* nor the instrumentation of *Nostalgie*, the harmony of *Bílá volavka* and the circular figurations of *Příznivá bouřka* have anything in common with Chinese culture. For that matter, Reisserová's musical style remains deeply rooted in the European sphere, unlike (for instance) that of Marguerite Canal, whose setting of seven poems from Toussaint's *La Flûte de Jade* "abounds with such ... exotic musical features."[266]

Reisserová confronted herself with two different musical worlds. During her studies in Prague and Bern, she was exposed to Germanic neoromantic music tinted with Czech ingredients. Then, upon her arrival in Paris, she discovered the impressionist school and its search for sound colors – achieved through

---

[265] Ralph P. Locke, *Musical Exoticism: Images and Reflections* (Cambridge: Cambridge University Press, 2011), 217.

[266] Hamer, *Female Composers*, 65.

modality (such as whole tone, and/or pentatonic scales), and instrumental timbres (including a celesta in *Jaro v ulici* and various percussion instruments) – and its twisting melodies. Nonetheless, she managed to digest all these cultural and technical influences into a coherent whole, which may not be as idiosyncratic as Roussel's, but which remains pleasant and emotional at all times. As the journalist of *Der Bund* wisely wrote, "in all her works there is a happy synthesis of the French spirit with Slavic melodicism,"[267] even though the concept of the "Slavic" still needs to be clearly defined.

6 Conclusion

"[H]er extensive cultural contacts and knowledge of foreign countries and art gave her a world orientation; few of our composers will enter the European stage as quickly as Reisserová did."[268]

Julie Reisserová was one of those rare women artists of the first third of the twentieth century to have had the good fortune to benefit from a privileged domestic situation. As the wife of a diplomat, she had adequate time to devote herself to her art, to deepen it with renowned masters, to build up a large culture according to her incessant travels across Europe, and to take advantage of influential contacts to have her music performed on the European and North American stages. This enviable social position undoubtedly enabled her to carve out a prominent place in a male-dominated world that was still very closed to women. By doing so, at a time when the participation of Czech women in musical life was limited,[269] she helped pave the way for other Czech women musicians, such as Vítězslava Kaprálová, and managed to become "a typical representative of the music of young, independent Czechoslovakia."[270]

In the current musicological literature, Reisserová exists almost exclusively through her links with Albert Roussel, and knowledge of her music is primarily based on the vocal score of the song cycle *Březen* and the three *Esquisses* for piano, published in Copenhagen. These two collections are indeed quite easily available in library shelves but offer only a meager sample of the production of the composer. Yet, the study of the *Pastorale maritimo*, probably Reisserová's most often performed symphonic opus, of *Pod sněhem* and of the *Suita*, enable

---

[267] *Der Bund* (March 17, 1938), 3: "So findet sich in allen ihren Werken eine glückliche Synthese des französischen Geistes mit der slawischen Melodik." See also Ursus, "Julie Reisserova," 19; and Hrdinová, "Julie Reisserová," 49.

[268] Heidenreich, "Za Julií Reisserovou," 94: "její rozsáhlé styky kulturní i poznání cizích zemí a umění, dalo jí orientaci světovou; málokdo z našich skladatelů vstoupí tak rychle na podium Evropy jako se to podařilo Reisserové."

[269] *Národní listy* (January 26, 1941), 5.

[270] Ursus, "Julie Reisserova," 19: "en typisk Repræsentant for Musiken i det unge, uafhængige Tjekoslovaki."

us to form a more accurate opinion of her art, in which the influence of Roussel, a certain romantic tradition, and an impressionist heritage are happily intertwined with so-called Czech feelings. As one critic rhetorically put it, in order to highlight the delicacy of her music and her ability not to renounce her Slavic heritage in the face of the Western model, "Mrs. Reisserová learned a lot from Albert Roussel, but she lost none of her delicacy of woman's soul, nor of her Slavic individuality."[271] Endowed with indisputable gifts, driven by the desire to make her country's music and culture better known in Western Europe and beyond, ready to defend the feminist cause alongside Františka Plamínková, and open to the world and to others, Julie Reisserová was a popular personality in her time.[272] However, in spite of her "Circle of Friends," she has remained overlooked, especially in Western Europe and in North America. This could be partly due to the difficult access to her scores, and to Czech domestic politics that affected her indirectly. Still, she deserves to regain the place she once occupied in the Czech musical pantheon.

---

[271] P. V., "Julie Reisserova," 515: "Mme Reisserova a beaucoup appris d'Albert Roussel, mais elle n'a rien perdu de sa finesse d'âme de femme, ni de son individualité slave."

[272] For a chronicler of *Lidové noviny* (November 28, 1944), 4, she was the most famous Czech female composer.

Appendix A: Vienna Lecture (1937)

The original text of the lecture Reisserová delivered in Vienna, "Die Frau als Komponistin," was written in German and is lost. Fortunately, large excerpts are reproduced in the May 1937 issue of *Die Österreicherin*, and the entire lecture was translated into Czech by Vacková.[1] The following translation is based on these German excerpts; the missing sentences and words are rendered from the complete Czech version available in Vacková's book and are put in brackets. Added material is placed in square brackets.

The Woman as Composer

(My topic is "The Woman as Composer." From this title alone it is clear that the woman composer is seen as an exceptional phenomenon. It is still widely believed that women lack the ability to express themselves creatively in music. However, I think that a great injustice is being done to women by this view.)

Music is the most immaterial of all arts, its world moves in dreamland. One could almost say that every musical work is surrealistic. Music is therefore the art that requires the greatest sensitivity from the author. And since it is generally acknowledged that the average woman has a greater sensitivity than the average man, this quality should be more of an advantage for her in the creation of music.

Nevertheless, it must be admitted that even today there are few women composers whose names are known. In my opinion, however, this state of affairs is not due to an innate lack of talent, but rather to historical development and social conditions.

(It was only the women's movement of the nineteenth century and the liberation of women in all fields of activity that won for them an equal position alongside men and the possibility of employment in the most diverse professions.)

It was not until the women's movement that women were able to assert themselves in a wide variety of professions. However, even before that there were important women writers and painters, but no well-known women composers. This is easy to explain.

Literary education has always been part of the "bon ton" of good society, as well as drawing and painting. Thus the basis for one's own creative work was prepared, provided that talent was available.[2] Of course, music lessons

---

[1] *Die Österreicherin*, 10th year, no. 4 (May 1937), 1–2; Vacková, *Julie Reisserová*, 49–52 ("Žena-skladatelka").

[2] Alternative Czech version: "In all schools and in private lessons – young girls were always taught the art of creation – but only if there was talent. But what about music?"

were also part of a good education. But what did one learn there? Violin or piano or singing. That is why there were also important virtuosos and singers. Here is the big difference. In literature and painting, women had always learned the basics for the productive, but in music only for the reproductive.

Such preparation was not enough for composing. Composition is unthinkable without a thorough study of theory. But music theory is a rigorous science, very close to mathematics and physics. And it was not until women began to study other exact sciences that they devoted themselves to this study. Today, many women study composition (in conservatories), and it can be assumed that in the near future we will meet more and more women as composers.

It would be a great mistake, however, if a woman were to compose only out of ambition, in order to equal a man in this profession as well. She should do it only when she feels the inner calling to do so, and her composition will be all the better the more sincere she is to herself. For art, in deep humility before all the wonders of creation, mercilessly condemns everything that is inauthentic. Art is absolutely indifferent to whether the creator is a man or a woman; the quality of talent alone is decisive for the resulting work of art.

(By talent I mean first of all creative ability, that is the grace of inspiration, when one is almost possessed by inner forces that directly dictate the creation of a new work; the creative imagination that tries to capture the dust of ideas that are seemingly unrelated and yet latently connected, that allows one to look beneath the existing world, beneath the real, and bring to light the mysterious relations of ideas; an intellectual acumen that distinguishes and sorts the good from the bad at the moment of creation, and which requires a refined technique of thinking.)

But creative talent alone is not enough to be able to compose. One must also learn composing as a *Métier* and master it in such a way that the creative is expressed, that the bubbling source of ideas is put into a form that makes the ideas comprehensible to the outside world. The greatest difficulty in creating music consists in writing it down, in the art of transforming the ideas of the ardent imagination into the visual notation in such a way that the real sound corresponds to the inner sound conception of the creator.

For this, the sovereign mastery of technique is necessary.

Acquiring this requires hard and difficult work. Many years of study are necessary to master harmony, counterpoint, formal theory, and instrumentation. (It must not be forgotten that this study is only a preparation for a profession that does not always sustain its master.) "To lead the many voices of the score in such a way that a work of art is created takes one's whole life," the French master Vincent d'Indy once claimed.[3]

(But there are things that cannot be taught. The skill can be developed. But this ability has to be there in order to even understand that such a large study is necessary. One could say, *cum grano salis*, that one must know before one begins to study. But for those who are like that, studying is doubly difficult.

Allow me a personal memory. When I came to Paris to Albert Roussel after my studies with J. B. Foerster in Prague, I considered myself an independent composer. When I played a piece for Roussel, he seemed very enthusiastic, and I thought he would allow me every liberty. But it was just the beginning! With his familiar, almost mathematical French logic and precision, he sat me down to a strict four-part chorale and made me write all the counterpoint problems [exercises] in the old keys. The solution had always to be musical, for Roussel could not bear to see mere theoretical handling of the voices even in exercises. It was the same with instrumentation, where I had to orchestrate Beethoven's and Schumann's piano works.

How overwhelming it was to see my imagination still being shackled by strict regulations. But the day came, after five years of what Roussel himself described as gymnastics of the brain, when he gave me my diploma. And it was after my first orchestral performance in Paris, when he said to me: "Vous voyez, la patience vient à bout à qui sait attendre" [*recte*: "tout vient à point à qui sait attendre": "See, good things come to those who wait."] Those lessons with Roussel remained unforgettable for me, for it was here that I understood the prerequisites of true art, that is, the eternally valid laws that every born artist follows almost instinctively, no matter which direction he follows, the laws that apply just as much to classical art as to modern art, just as much to the revolutionary as to the traditionalist.[4]

---

[3] Alternative Czech version: "I once asked the French Master Vincent d'Indy how many years he thought one should study composition if one was to master everything. 'Twelve years,' he said. And seeing my surprise, he explained further: 'Two years a roofer needs to learn his trade, or he would fall off the roof. A pearl-stringer needs even more time to know how to arrange pearls according to their size and lustre. It takes a lifetime to learn how to arrange the many voices of a score to create a work of art.'"

[4] German version: "Only devoted study allows us to recognize the preconditions of true art. That is to say, the eternally valid laws according to which every born artist almost instinctively acts, no matter which direction he follows, the laws that apply to classical art as well as to modern art, to the revolutionary as well as to the traditionalist." This echoes Reisserová's statement in E. K., "Z rozhovorů s Julii Reisserovou," 4: "I don't like to use the word 'modern.' If a new work is strong, it is always modern, or always 'timeless.' Nowadays, the word modern only accentuates temporality too much. The desire is not to create a work according to a modern recipe, but to create a work so strong that it itself determines the modern direction." ("Zásadně nerada užívám slovo 'moderní.' Je-li nové dílo silné, je vždy moderní, resp. vždy 'nečasové.' Dnes slovem moderní se příliš akcentuje jen časovost. Nemá se toužit po tom, aby se dílo udělalo podle moderního receptu, nýbrž po tom, aby se vytvořilo dílo tak silné, že by ono samo určilo moderní směr.")

But I can assure you that I have sometimes asked myself whether I will always have the necessary strength to keep up with the formidable competition and the breakneck pace of modern times. Everything in this profession requires a great deal of self-denial, more so for a woman than for a man.)

Composing also requires great self-overcoming, especially for a woman. For example, when a woman stands in front of the orchestra for the first time at a rehearsal of her own work, she feels how all the people look at her with a mixture of politeness, mistrust, and ridicule. In front of an orchestra, only skill counts; even women can only impress with their musicality. That is where Goethe's well-known word comes into its own: "To be conscious of one's art everywhere" ["Sich seiner Kunst überall bewußt zu sein"]. To reach this height, the composer needs something else besides talent and mastery of technique: a great vitality. For this is a profession that consumes the whole soul and the whole person. It is only the love of art, this sacred flame that keeps one high, but at the same time consumes one.

(I am referring to the process of creating a work. Something is happening in the laboratory of the brain that no one has yet been able to put into words.) Like every author, I have been asked several times how the ideas actually come. And like every author I have to answer that in such moments one feels like a medium through which an unknown power speaks. Pfitzner expressed it best. In the scene of his opera *Palestrina*, as the angels dictate his famous mass to the old master, he says simply: "It is just as incomprehensible and mysterious as birth." ["Es ist geradeso unbegreiflich und geheimnisvoll wie die Geburt."]

(It is a gift from the Danaids. But whom art has marked as its spokesman, he will not escape his fate. However, I would not like to give you the impression that I see only difficulties in this profession.) The artist's path is a way of the cross, but there are also moments of redemption, moments of creation, of purest joy, as the enchanted soul grasps the true meaning of those words that Schubert so heavenly set to music: "O blessed art, I thank you." ["Du holde Kunst / Ich danke dir."][5]

---

[5] Franz Schubert, Franz von Schober, *An die Musik*, D 547.

Appendix B: Catalog of Musical Works

1 – *Březen* (*Giboulées de Mars*; *März*; *Marts*); 1923–1925

   (i) Photostatic edition: [Copenhagen]: Atelier Elektra, n.d. [ca. 1934?]
Three known copies: Royal Danish Library, Copenhagen, KB Victor Albecks Vej, Aarhus 4–92–5313; Den Sorte Diamant, U208 1935–36.112. Library of the Conservatoire régional du Grand-Nancy (France), 490 REI

   (ii) *Březen, cyklus písní s orkestrem Klavírní výtah prof. Emil Hájek.* Copenhagen: Skandinavisk og Borups Musikforlag, 1934
- *Za svítání* (*À l'aube*; *In der Frühe*; *Ved Gry*) [Eduard Mörike], dedicated to Marie Žaludová
- *Nostalgie* (*Nostalgi*) [Ōshikōchi no Mitsune], dedicated to Zdeňka Ziková
- *Jaro v ulici* (*Printemps dans la rue*; *Frühling in der Strasse*; *Foraar i Gaden*) [Julie Reisserová], dedicated to Anna Klecandová-Martenová
- *Světlo* (*Lumière*; *Das Licht*; *Lyset*) [Julie Reisserová], dedicated to Vojtěch Kühnl

2 – *Suita*; Original title: *Letní den*; 1924–1931

   Dedicated to Albert Roussel

   Photostatic edition: [Copenhagen]: Atelier Elektra, n.d. [ca. 1934?]

   Three known copies: Royal Danish Library, Copenhagen, KB Victor Albecks Vej, Aarhus 4–92–5312; Den Sorte Diamant, U150 1935–36.113. Library of the Conservatoire régional du Grand-Nancy (France), 490 REI
- *Allegro giocoso*; 1930–1931
- *Andantino espressivo*; 1930–1931
- *Allegro con moto*; original title: *La Bise*; 1924–1929

3 – *Esquisses, piano solo*; 1928–1932

   Print: Copenhagen: Skandinavisk og Borups Musikforlag, 1935
- *Allegro deciso*; 1932; dedicated to Aline van Bärentzen
- *Adagio meditativo*; 1932; dedicated to Emil Hájek
- *Allegro giocoso e ben ritmico*; original title: *Allégresse*; 1928; dedicated to Denyse Molié

4 – *Pastorale maritimo*; 1933

   Dedicated to Madame Albert Roussel

(i) Autograph manuscript: Library of the Conservatoire régional du Grand-Nancy (France), no call-number

(ii) Photostatic edition: [Copenhagen]: Atelier Elektra, n.d. [ca. 1934–1935]

Only one known copy: Library of the Conservatoire régional du Grand-Nancy (France), 490 REI

(iii) Set of fourteen parts: [Copenhagen]: Atelier Elektra, n.d. [ca. 1934–1935]

Only one known incomplete set (double-bass part missing): Library of the Conservatoire régional du Grand-Nancy (France), no call-number

(iv) Handwritten string parts copied out at Nancy in 1936:[1] Library of the Conservatoire régional du Grand-Nancy (France), no call-number

5 – *Pod sněhem, Čínská poesie* (*Sous la neige*); ca. 1934–1937

Non-autograph manuscript: University of Michigan Music Library, Women Composers Collection WCC 2662

- *Vzpomínka* (*Souvenir*; *Erinnerung*) [Li Tai Po] dedicated to Inger Raasløff
- *Bílá volavka* (*Le Héron blanc*; *Der weisse Reiher*) [Li Tai Po] dedicated to Elšlégravá Puklová
- *Přízniva bouřka* (*L'Orage favorable*; *Das gute Unwetter*) [Tsao Chang Ling] dedicated to Else Schøtt

6 –*Slavnostní den, ženský sbor*; 1935

Dedicated to Františka Plamínková

Photostatic edition: [Copenhagen]: Atelier Elektra, n.d. [ca. 1935]

Only one known copy: Royal Danish Library, Copenhagen: KB Victor Albecks Vej, Aarhus 4–92–4854

Poem by the composer

7 – *Předjaří* (*Février*; *Februar*; *Vorfrühling*); 1936

Dedicated to Maria Jensen-Milliet

Non-autograph manuscript (now lost) whose first page is reproduced in Vacková, *Julie Reisserová*, 3.

Poem by Werner Rudolf Beer

8 – Miscellanea

- Overture to *Poledního údělu* (*Partage de midi* by Paul Claudel) for large orchestra; ca. 1919?–1931 (lost)

---

[1] The invoice was paid on March 10, 1936, for the 1935 fiscal year. Library of the Conservatoire régional du Grand-Nancy, no call-number.

- *Pramen* (*La Source*); ca. 1927 (lost piano piece)
- *Vítr* (*Le Vent*); ca. 1927 (lost piano piece)
- *Jarní*; ca. 1928 (lost song)
- *Dva mužské sbory* (*Two male choirs*); 1929 (lost)
- String Quartet; ca. 1931 (unrealized project?)
- Violin Sonata; ca. 1931 (unrealized project?)
- *Deux Allegros pro Klavír* [*Allegro inquieto*; *Allegro diabolico*]; ca. 1934? (lost)
- Piano Concerto; ca. 1937 (unrealized project)

Appendix C: List of Documented Public Performances of Reisserová's Music

List compiled from Vacková's book, Montagnier's article "Autour de la *Pastorale maritimo*," and the international press. Data are given in the following order: date; place; work title(s); performer(s); source(s) when the concert is not mentioned by Vacková and/or Montagnier, or when information is contradictory.

1927

- Unknown date (March?); Bern; *Za svítání*, *Světlo*, *La Bise*; M. Strack (soprano), Ernst Hohlfeld (conductor)
- January 31; Lucerne (Theater); *La Bise*; Ballet of the Prague National Theater, Lydia Wisiaková (dancer)
- February 24; Paris ("Université Alexandre Mercereau"); *Za svítání*; Zdeňka Krausová (soprano), Libuše Nováková (piano)
- March 7; Paris (La Sorbonne); "Dvě melodie," *Pramen*; Jeanne Bathori (soprano), Jane Mortier (piano), Julie Reisserová (piano accompaniment); *La Semaine à Paris*, no. 249 (March 4–11, 1927), 36; *Národní listy* (March 31, 1927), 9
- March 17; Paris (salle Pleyel); *Za svítání*, *Nostalgie*, *Světlo*; Zdeňka Krausová, Jane Mortier
- November 16; Prague (Mozarteum); *Za svítání*, *Světlo*; Marie Bodláková (soprano), O. Ferrarotti (piano)

1928

- March 24; Paris (Schola Cantorum); *Za svítání*; Artur Gofmann (tenor), Libuše Nováková or Julie Reisserová (piano accompaniment)?; *La Semaine à Paris* (March 23–30, 1928), 92; *Národní listy* (April 6, 1928), 4
- April 28; Geneva (Club international); *Za svítání*, *Světlo*; Julie Reisserová, Marie Jansenová; *Le Journal de Genève* (April 29, 1928), 6
- May 4; Bern; *Za svítání*, *Nostalgie*, *Světlo*; Marie Jansen[ová] (soprano), Julie Reisserová (piano accompaniment); *Der Bund* (May 7, 1928), 3
- June 30; Montreux (Casino); *La Bise*; Thermal baths orchestra
- July 14 (June?); Montreux (Casino); *Allégresse* (*Esquisses* no. 3); Denyse Molié (piano)
- November 1; Montreux (Casino); *La Bise*; Thermal baths orchestra

1929

- March 22; Bern; *Nostalgie, Jaro v ulici, Světlo, Allégresse*; Jeanne Bathori (soprano), Denyse Molié
- March 23; Bern; *Allégresse*; Denyse Molié
- April 16; Paris (La Sorbonne); *Za svítání*; Zdeňka Krausová, Denyse Molié
- April 23; Paris (salle Gaveau); *La Bise, Nostalgie, Jaro v ulici*; Lydia de Rivera (soprano), Orchestre du Conservatoire, Marius-François Gaillard (conductor)

1930

- April 2; Bern; *Nostalgie, Jaro v ulici*; Violette Andreosi (soprano), Bern Orchestra, Albert Neff (conductor)
- April 5; Bern; *Jaro v ulici*; Berthe de Vigier (soprano)
- November 21; Prague; *Březen, Allégresse*; Marie Zupancová (soprano), Erwin Schulhoff (piano)
- November; Paris (Concert organized by Anna Klecandová-Martenová); ?; ?; *Národní listy* (November 26, 1930), 5

1931

- May 14; Belgrade; *Za svítání, Nostalgie, Světlo, Allégresse*; Marie Žaludová-Knittlová (soprano), Emil Hájek (piano), Julie Reisserová (piano accompaniment)
- October 23; Prague (Lucerna); *Březen, Suita*; Czech Philharmonic Orchestra, Pavel Dědeček (conductor), Marie Žaludová-Knittlová

1932

- February 7; Prague (and Radio-Praha); *Březen, Suita*; Marie Zupancová, Otakar Jeremiáš (conductor)
- February 8; Belgrade; *Allégresse*; Emil Hájek; *Prager Presse* (February 9, 1932), 5
- April 23; Belgrade; *Jaro v ulici, Allégresse*; Marie Žaludová-Knittlová, Emil Hájek
- May 29 (30?); Prague (Radio-Praha); *Esquisses*; Erwin Schulhoff; *Le Progrès de la Côte-d'Or* (May 30, 1932), 4

1933

- April 23; Belgrade; *Suita*; Belgrade Philharmonic Orchestra, Stefan Hristić (conductor)
- May 2; Belgrade; *Jaro v ulici, Světlo*; Aša Slavická (soprano)
- May 9; Paris (Salle Gaveau and Poste Parisien); *Nostalgie, Jaro v ulici* (piano or symphonic version?); Orchestre du Poste Parisien, Théodore Mathieu (conductor), Pia Igy (soprano), Maurice Béché (piano accompaniment); *La*

Semaine à Paris (May 5–12, 1933), [58]; *Le Peuple* (May 8, 1933), 2; *Excelsior* (May 8, 1933), [6]; *Chicago Daily Tribune: European Edition* (May 11, 1933), 4; *Le Journal* (May 21, 1933), 7
- September 17?; Belgrade; *Pastorale maritimo*; Belgrade Philharmonic Orchestra

1934
- February–March; Tour in Scandinavian countries; *Březen, Pastorale maritimo*; Alice Raveau (soprano); *Národní listy večerník* (April 7, 1934), 3; *Národní politika* (April 7, 1934), 8
- February 10; Paris; *Za svítání*; Alice Raveau, Édouard Gendron (piano)
- February 17; Copenhagen (French Embassy); *Za svítání*; Alice Raveau
- February–March; Copenhagen; *Březen, Pastorale maritimo*; Alice Raveau, Copenhagen Philharmonic Orchestra, Nicolai Malko (conductor); *Národní listy* (April 7, 1934), 3; *Národní politika* (April 7, 1934), 8
- March 2; Copenhagen; *Za svítání, Světlo*; Inger Raasløff (soprano), Christian Christiansen (piano)
- March 2; Copenhagen (Danish Radio); *Allégresse*; Emil Hájek
- March 3; Copenhagen; *Esquisses*; Emil Hájek
- March 7; Copenhagen; *Světlo, Allégresse*; Else Schøtt (soprano), Emil Hájek
- April 29; Prague (Vinohrady Theater); *Pastorale maritimo, Březen, Esquisses*; Zdeňka Ziková (soprano), Orchestra of the Prague Conservatory, Pavel Dědeček, Emil Hájek
- June 6; Copenhagen (Tivoli); *Pastorale maritimo*; Svend Christian Felumb (conductor)
- July 29; Copenhagen; *Allégresse*; Emil Hájek
- August 6; Copenhagen (Tivoli); *Esquisses*; Emil Hájek
- August 22; Copenhagen (Tivoli); *Březen*; Zdeňka Ziková, Svend Christian Felumb
- October 16; Prague (Smetana Hall); *Světlo*; Zdeňka Ziková, Erivan Meller (piano); *Národní listy* (October 6, 1934), 4; *Národní politika* (October 8, 1934), 4
- October 23; Prague (Lucerna); *Světlo*; Zdeňka Ziková, Erivan Meller
- November 12; Prague; *Světlo*; Else Schøtt, Oldřich Letfus (piano)
- December 11; Vienna; *Světlo*; Zdeňka Ziková, Erivan Meller

1935
- January 22; Copenhagen (Czechoslovak Embassy); *Březen*; Inger Raasløff, Leo Demant (piano)
- February 4; Prague (Urania Palace); *Esquisses*; Emil Hájek; *Prager Presse* (February 6, 1935), 6

- March 2; Copenhagen; *Březen*; Julie Nessyová-Bächerová (soprano), Fritz Busch (conductor)
- March 6; Copenhagen; *Světlo*; Julie Nessyová-Bächerová, Felix de Nobel (conductor? piano?)
- March 7; Copenhagen (Czechoslovak Embassy); *Březen, Esquisses* no. 2; Inger Raasløff, Leo Demant
- March 18; Copenhagen; *Za svítání, Světlo*; Marie Hussa (soprano), Walter Meyer-Radon (piano)
- April 12; Olomouc; *Suita*; Theater Orchestra and members of the Prostějov Orchestral Association, Adolf Heller (conductor)
- May 13; Prague (Radio-Praha); *Esquisses*; Erwin Schulhoff
- May 27; Vienna (Radio-Wien); *Pastorale maritimo*; Funkorchester der Wiener Symphoniker, Josef Holzer (conductor); *Innsbrucker Rachrichten* (May 24, 1935), 7
- September 4; Vichy (Parc des Sources); *Pastorale maritimo*; Orchestra of the festival, Louis Fourestier (conductor)
- September 18; Copenhagen (broadcast live on Radio-Wien and the Danish Radio); *Březen*; Else Schøtt, Denmark Radio Symphony Orchestra, Nikolai Malko (conductor)
- November 8; Copenhagen; *Světlo*; Else Schøtt, J. Kjær (piano)
- November 18; Bratislava (Radio); *Pastorale maritimo*; Radio Orchestra?, Adolf Heller; *Antena* (November 17, 1935), xii.
- November 19; Prague (Radio-Praha); *Suita*; Otakar Jeremiáš
- November 22; Copenhagen; *Za svítání, Světlo*; Elisabeth Jürgens (soprano), Willy Klassen (conductor)
- December 7; Copenhagen; *Březen*; Else Schøtt, Christian Christiansen
- December 10; Copenhagen (Czechoslovak Embassy); *Světlo*; Else Schøtt, Leo Demant
- December 10; Bratislava (Radio); *Pastorale maritimo*; Radio Orchestra, Adolf Heller; *Antena* (December 8, 1935), xvi

1936

- January 16; Copenhagen; *Za svítání*; *Světlo*; Inger Raasløff, Hans Hammer (piano)
- January 18; Karlovy Vary (Carlsbad); *Pastorale maritimo*; Thermal baths orchestra, Robert Manzer (conductor)
- January 22; Prague (Social Club); *Březen*; Alena Pečírková (soprano), Václav Štěpán (piano)

- February 14; Aarhus; *Esquisses* no. 1, *Světlo*; Rudolf Firkušný (piano), Else Schøtt, Hans Meyer-Petersen (piano accompaniment); *Prager Presse* (February 13, 1936), 5
- February 15; Aalborg; *Esquisses* no. 1, *Světlo*; Rudolf Firkušný (piano), Else Schøtt, Hans Meyer-Petersen (piano accompaniment)
- February 16; Nancy (salle Victor Poirel); *Pastorale maritimo*; Orchestre du Conservatoire, Alfred Bachelet (conductor)
- February 18; Copenhagen; *Esquisses* no. 1; Rudolf Firkušný
- March 14; Bern; *Světlo, Esquisses* no. 1; Maria Jensen-Milliet, Hedi Durrer (piano)
- March 15; Vienna (Ravag; Radio-Wien); *Pastorale maritimo*; Wiener Symphoniker, Bruno Pleier (conductor)
- April 29; Copenhagen; *Allégresse*; France Ellegaard (piano)
- May 13; Copenhagen (Tivoli); *Světlo*; Elsa Schøtt, Tivolis Koncertsals Orkester, Svend Christian Felumb
- June 18; Copenhagen; *Za svítání*; E. de Koriakine, Frizt Crome
- June 22; Copenhagen; *Za svítání, Světlo, Esquisses* no. 2; Inger Raasløff, Helge Nørgaard (piano), Alexander Borovsky (piano)
- June 26; Copenhagen (Tivoli); *Pastorale maritimo*; Tivolis Koncertsals Orkester, Svend Christian Felumb; *Lidové noviny* (July 23, 1936), 9
- July 1; Radio-Strasbourg/Paris; *Pastorale maritimo*; Henri Tomasi; *De Standaard* (July 1, 1936), 6; *L'Écho de Sélestat* (July 1, 1936), [4]; *Lidové noviny* (July 23, 1936), 9
- July 26; Prague (Radio concert from Karlovy Vary); *Suita*; Thermal baths orchestra, Robert Manzer (conductor)
- July 29; Riga (Radio); *Esquisses* no. 2; Leo Demant
- September 11; Prague (Společenský klub); *Pod sněhem*; Gilberte Arvez-Vernet (soprano), Aline van Bärentzen (piano)
- September 12; Prague (Lucerna); *Březen*; Gilberte Arvez-Vernet; Czech Philharmonic Orchestra, Karel Boleslav Jirák (conductor)
- September 14; Prague (Radio-Praha); *Esquisses*; Aline van Bärentzen
- November 7; Karlovy Vary; *Suita*; Thermal baths orchestra, Robert Manzer
- November 20; Prague; *Pod sněhem*; Inger Raasløff, Hans Walter Süsskind (piano)
- November 24; Prague; *Pod sněhem, Březen*; Inger Raasløff, Václav Holzknecht (piano)
- November 30; Prague (Lucerna); *Světlo*; Máša Kolárová (soprano), Josef Kunstadt (piano)
- December 15; Radio-Normandie; *Esquisses, Březen*; Gilberte Arvez-Vernet, Julie Reisserová (piano accompaniment)

1937

- January 15; Craiova (as part of a tour in Romania); *Březen*; Pia Igy; *Prager Presse* (January 27, 1937), 7; *Prager Presse* (January 29, 1937), 8; *Národní listy* (February 2, 1937), 5
- ?; Budapest; *Pastorale maritimo*; Budapest Symphony Orchestra; *Le Guide du Concert* (February 12, 1937), 515
- ? January; Radio-Normandie; *Březen*; Gilberte Arvez-Vernet
- ? January; Radio-Normandie; *Esquisses*; Julien Pouyer (piano)
- January 13; Zurich (Music Academy); *Světlo*, *Předjaří*, *Esquisses* no. 1; Maria Jensen-Milliet, Hedi Durrer
- January 21; Vienna (Ravag [Radio]); *Březen*; Eva Hadrabová (soprano)
- January 28; Paris (salle Pleyel); *Pastorale maritimo*; Orchestre de la Société Philharmonique, Charles Munch (conductor)
- ? February; Paris (Radio); *Pod sněhem*; Gilberte Arvez-Vernet
- February 12; Copenhagen; *Pod sněhem*; Inger Raasløff, Christian Christiansen
- February 16; Paris (Revue musicale); *Pod sněhem*, *Březen*, *Esquisses*; Gilberte Arvez-Vernet, Aline van Bärentzen, Julie Reisserová (piano accompaniment); *L'Art musical* (February 26, 1937), 503
- February 16; Riga (Radio); *Allégresse*; France Ellegaard
- February 18; Helsinki (Radio); *Allégresse*; France Ellegaard
- February 22; Copenhagen; *Pod sněhem*; Inger Raasløff, Christian Christiansen
- February 23; Prague; *Esquisses*; Marie Tarantová (piano)
- February 24; Prague; *Esquisses* no. 2; Alexander Borovsky (piano)
- March 3; Bratislava; *Březen*; Milada Jirásková (soprano)
- March 10; Copenhagen; *Esquisses* no. 1; Rudolf Firkušný
- March 17; Brussels (Bärentzen's home); *Březen*, *Pod sněhem*, *Esquisses* no. 1; Gilberte Arvez-Vernet, Julie Reisserová (piano accompaniment), Aline van Bärentzen
- March 19; Radio-Strasbourg; *Pastorale maritimo*, *Březen*; Gilberte Arvez-Vernet, Maurice de Villers (conductor); *Der Elsässer* (March 12, 1937), [6]; *Der Republikaner* (March 13, 1937), [10]; *Lidové noviny* (March 14, 1937), 7
- April 8; Strasbourg (Radio-Strasbourg); *Esquisses*; Aline van Bärentzen
- April 23; Vienna (House of Industry); *Březen*, *Pod sněhem*, *Esquisses*; Maria Hussa (soprano), Aline van Bärentzen
- April 26; Vienna (Radio-Wien); *Esquisses* no. 1, *Allégresse*; Aline van Bärentzen; *Radio Wien* (April 23, 1937), 14; *Rundfunkbeilage des Pester Lloyd* (April 24, 1937), 24

- July 28; Paris (Radio-Paris); *Pod sněhem*; Gilberte Arvez-Vernet; *Le Matin* (July 28, 1937), 6; *La Meuse* (July 28, 1937), 9; *L'Ordre* (July 28, 1937), 4
- October 30; Paris (Radio Tour-Eiffel); *Pod sněhem*; Gilberte Arvez-Vernet; *Le Journal* (October 29, 1937), 4; *Laatste Nieuws* (October 29, 1937), 12; *Ce Soir* (October 30, 1937), 9
- December 3; Prague; *Slavnostní den*; Singing Association of Prague Female Teachers, Metod Vymetal (conductor)
- ?; Moravská Ostrava (Radio); *Březen*; Anna Stračovská-Černíková (soprano), Erwin Schulhoff

1938

- End of January?; Philadelphia; *Slavnostní den*; The Montgomery Singers, Lela Vauclain (conductor)?
- ?; Copenhagen; *Pod sněhem*; Inger Raasløff; *Národní politika* (February 1, 1938), 7
- April 11; Copenhagen (Danmarks Radio); *Suita, Pastorale maritimo, Světlo, Pod sněhem*; Danmarks Radio Orchestra, Erik Tuxen (conductor), Inger Raasløff, Folmer Jensen (piano); *Nationen* (April 9, 1938), 10
- April 26; Prague; *Pod sněhem, Březen, Slavnostní den*; Zdeňka Ziková, Hans Walter Süsskind, Singing Association of Prague Female Teachers; *Národní listy* (April 22, 1938), 2; *Lidové noviny* (April 26, 1938), 10; *Prager Presse* (April 28, 1938), 7
- April 26; Paris (Revue musicale); *Pod sněhem, Březen*; Gilberte Arvez-Vernet, Maroussia Orloff (piano)
- April 28; Paris (École normale de musique); *La Bise* (piano version), *Esquisses, Březen, Pod sněhem, Předjaří*; O. Guerfort (soprano; she replaced Aimée Félix who was ill), Aline van Bärentzen, Mrs. Blanchard de Chatillon (piano accompaniment), Marie Tymichová (who danced in *La Bise*)
- June 2; Paris (Radio Paris-Mondial); *Pod sněhem*; ?; *Le Journal* (June 2, 1938), 6
- ? October; Prague; *Pod sněhem*; Jindra Schurzová (soprano); *Národní politika* (October 21, 1938), 6; *Prager Presse* (October 22, 1938), 7
- December 30; Belgrade; *Březen*; Zdeňka Ziková, MihailoVukdragović (conductor); *Lidové noviny* (January 30, 1938), 10; *Národní politika* (February 1, 1938), 7

1939

- January; Prague; *Esquisses*; Anna Kremarová (piano); *Národní listy* (January 27, 1939), 3

1940

- February 23; Prague; *Pod sněhem, Březen, Esquisses*; Marie Zupancová-Reisserová [Bodláková-Reisserová], Otakar Vondrovic (piano); *Lidové noviny* (February 25, 1940), 9
- May 15; Prague (Radio-Praha); ?; ?; *Lidové noviny* (May 15, 1940), 4

1941

- February 25; Prague; *Pod sněhem, Březen, Esquisses*; Marie [Bodláková-]Reisserová, Julie Wildová-Maxiánová (soprano), Otakar Vondrovic; *Lidové noviny* (February 27, 1941), 7; *Venkov* (February 27, 1941), 7
- May 15; Prague; *Pod sněhem, Březen, Esquisses*; Marie [Bodláková-]Reisserová, Julie Wildová-Maxiánová, Otakar Vondrovic; *Národní listy* (March 8, 1941), 4; *Lidové noviny* (March 15, 1941), 7; *Ženská rada*, 17th year, no. 4 (April 26, 1941), 70; *Lidové noviny* (May 12, 1941), 2

1948

- February 22; Prague (radio); *Březen*; Drahomíra Tikalová (soprano); *Náš rozhlas* (February 22, 1948), 14

1949

- November 16; Rio de Janeiro (Municipal Theater); *Jaro v ulici*; Marie Bodláková-Reisserová, Otto Jordan (piano); *Diario Carioca* (November 10, 1949), 6; *Jornal do Brasil* (November 11, 1949), 10; *Correio da Manhã* (November 18, 1949), 15

1950

- March 27; Petropólis (Dom Pedro Theater); *Jaro v ulici*?; Marie Bodláková-Reisserová, Dinie Meyer (piano); *A Manhã* (March 29, 1950), 3

Select Bibliography

References cited only once and newspaper titles are not listed unless they are directly related to Julie Reisserová.

Bernard, Robert, "Musiques diverses pour piano." In *La Revue musicale*, vol. 17, no. 169 (November 1936), 367–368.

Brejcha, Miroslav, "Československy diplomat JUDr: Robert Flieder," unpublished PhD dissertation, Charles University, 2006.

Březina, Aleš, "Albert Roussel a jeho česká přátelství." In *Harmonie* (August 2017), 4–5.

Černušák, Gracian, Bohumír Štědroň, and Zdenko Nováček (eds.), *Československý hudební slovník osob a institucí*. Prague: Státní hudební nakladatelství, 1963–1965.

Chastain, André, "Une compositrice tchèque: Mme Julie Reisserova au Festival de Vichy." In *Comœdia* (September 13, 1935), 5.

Čornej, Petr, *Historici, historiografie a dějepis: Studie, črty, eseje*. Prague: Univerzita Karlova v Praze, 2016.

"Dotazník." In "Reisserová" folder, Center for Music Lexicography in Brno, no call-number.

Dumesnil, René, "Julie Reisserova." In *Mercure de France* (June 1, 1938), 457.

E. K., "Z rozhovorů s Julii Reisserovou." In *Národní politika: Odpolední vydání* (October 20, 1931), 4.

Gates, Eugene, "The Woman Composer Question: Philosophical and Historical Perspectives." In Eugene Gates and Karla Hartl (eds.), *The Women in Music Anthology*. Toronto: The Kapralova Society, 2021, 3–29.

Green, Lucy, *Music, Gender, Education*. Cambridge: Cambridge University Press, 1997.

Hamer, Laura, *Female Composers, Conductors, Performers: Musiciennes of Interwar France, 1919–1939*. New York: Routledge, 2018.

Heidenreich, Julius [J. H. H.], "Za Julií Reisserovou." In *Československo-jihoslovanská revue* vol. 8, nos. 3–4 (1938), 94.

Holečková-Heidenreichová, Jelena, "Za Julií Reisserovou." In *Ženská rada*, 14th year, no. 4 (April 1938), 60–63, 79–80.

Hrdinová, Josefa, "Julie Reisserová." In *Škola a rodina*, 5th year, year 1931–1932 (December 1931), 49.

Hrdinová, Josefa, "Julie Reisserová: Osobnost a život." In *Kulturní letáky: Musea a studijního ústavu odborných škol pro ženská povoláni v Praze*.

Prague: Ústav pro učebné pomůcky odborných a průmyslových škol, [1941], [1]–[2].

Le Flem, Paul, "Un concert d'ouvrages inédits." In *Comœdia* (April 28, 1929), 2.

Mondésir, Élisabeth de, "Hommage à J. Reisserova." In *L'Art musical* (May 6, 1938), 780–781.

Montagnier, Jean-Paul C., "Autour de la *Pastorale maritimo* de Julie Reisserová (1888–1938)." In *Revue belge de musicologie*, LXXIV (2020), 143–166.

Montagnier, Jean-Paul C. (ed.), *Julie Reisserová: Œuvres pour orchestre/Orchestral Works. Suita, Pastorale maritimo*. Berlin: Ries & Erler, 2022.

Montagnier, Jean-Paul C., "Julie Reisserová (1888–1938): A Czech Woman Composer of Importance." In Sabine Meine and Kaï Hinrich Müller (eds.), *It's a Man's World? Künstlerinnen in Europas Musik-Metropolen des frühen 20. Jahrhunderts*. Würzburg: Königshausen & Neumann GmbH, 2023, 157–167.

Montagnier, Jean-Paul C. (ed.), *Julie Reisserová: Březen. Version pour orchestre/Orchestral Version*. Berlin: Ries & Erler, 2023.

Montagnier, Jean-Paul C. (ed.), *Julie Reisserová: Musique de chambre/Chamber Music. Březen-Giboulées de mars, Pod sněhem-Sous la neige, Slavnostní den-Jour de fête, Esquisses pour piano*. Berlin: Ries & Erler, 2023.

Pellé, J. M., "Julie Reisserová v Paříži." In *Národní sjednocení* (February 12, 1937), 5.

Launay, Florence, *Les compositrices en France au xixe siècle*. Paris: Fayard, 2006.

P. V., "Julie Reisserova." In *Le Guide du Concert* (February 12, 1937), 515.

Solie, Ruth A., "Culture, Feminism, and the Sacred: Sophie Drinker's Musical Activism." In Ralph P. Locke and Cyrilla Barr (eds.), *Cultivating Music in America: Women Patrons and Activists since 1860*. Berkeley: University of California Press, 1997, 266–288.

Stefan, Paul, "Viennese Festival Weeks begin auspiciously." In *Musical America* (July 1937), 22.

Stf., P., "Julie Reisserova gestorben." In *Die Stunde* (March 3, 1938), 3.

Stf., P., "Julie Reisserova über die Frau als Komponistin." In *Die Stunde* (April 27, 1937), 4.

Upton, George Putnam, *Woman in Music*. Chicago: A. C. McClurg and Company, 1892.

Urban, Gisela, "Komponistin und Diplomatenfrau: Julie Reißerova in Wien." In *Neues Wiener Journal* (April 20, 1937), 7.

Ursus, "Julie Reisserova." In *Forum* (February 29, 1936), 19.

Vacková, Jiřina, "Hudební tvorba Julie Reisserové." In *Kulturní letáky: Musea a studijního ústavu odborných škol pro ženská povoláni v Praze*. Prague: Ústav pro učebné pomůcky odborných a průmyslových škol, [1941], [2]–[4].

Vacková, Jiřina, *Julie Reisserová: Osobnost a dílo*. Prague: A. J. Boháč, 1948.

Vacková, Jiřina, "Ó, božské umění, děkuji ti!" In *Lidové noviny* (October 9, 1993), vii.

Vedral, Vaclav, "In memoriam Julija Reisserova." In *Muzički glasnik*, 4 (1938), 83.

Závada, Vilém, "Skladatelka Julie Reisserová o sobě." In *Rozpravy Aventina*, vol. 7, no. 6 (October 5, 1931), 44–45.

W. R. B., "Julia Reißerova." In *Der Bund* (March 17, 1938), 3.

Acknowledgments

I thank Miriam Blümlová, Claire Fontijn, Karla Hartl, Petr Macek, Greta Morris, Laurent Schmitt, Ana Stefanovic, Damien Top, the staff of the institutions mentioned in the present contribution, and the members of the German-Czech research program *Musica non grata*.

Cambridge Elements

Women in Music

Rhiannon Mathias
Bangor University

Dr. Rhiannon Mathias is Lecturer and Music Fellow in the School of Music and Media at Bangor University. She is the author of a number of women in music publications, including *Lutyens, Maconchy, Williams and Twentieth-Century British Music: A Blest Trio of Sirens* (2012), and gives frequent conference presentations, public lectures and radio broadcasts on the topic. She is also the editor of the Routledge Handbook on *Women's Work in Music*, a publication which arose from the First International Conference on Women's Work in Music (Bangor University, 2017), which she instigated and directed. The success of the first conference led to her directing a second conference in 2019.

About the Series

Elements in Women in Music provides an exciting and timely resource for an area of music scholarship which is undergoing rapid growth. The subject of music, women and culture is widely researched in the academy, and has also recently become the focus of much public debate in mainstream media.

This international series will bring together many different strands of research on women in classical and popular music. Envisaged as a multimedia digital 'stage' for showcasing new perspectives and writing of the highest quality, the series will make full use of online materials such as music sound links, audio and/or film materials (e.g. performances, interviews – with permission), podcasts and discussion forums relevant to chosen themes.

The series will appeal primarily to music students and scholars, but will also be of interest to music practitioners, industry professionals, educators and the general public.

Cambridge Elements

Women in Music

Elements in the Series

Grażyna Bacewicz, The 'First Lady of Polish Music'
Diana Ambache

Leokadiya Kashperova: Biography, 'Memoirs' and 'Recollections of Anton Rubinstein'
Graham Griffiths

Julie Reisserová (1888–1938): Czech Composer and Feminist
Jean-Paul C. Montagnier

A full series listing is available at: www.cambridge.org/EWIM

For EU product safety concerns, contact us at Calle de José Abascal, 56–1°,
28003 Madrid, Spain or eugpsr@cambridge.org.

www.ingramcontent.com/pod-product-compliance
Lightning Source LLC
LaVergne TN
LVHW020350260326
834688LV00045B/1637